Raleigh

The Statue of the Presidents stands before the east entrance of the Capitol. It was done by Charles Keck to honor the three American Presidents from the State of North Carolina, James K. Polk of Mecklenburg County, Andrew Jackson of Union County, and Andrew Johnson of Wake County. Dedication ceremonies took place in 1948 and were attended by President Harry S. Truman.

Courtesy of North Carolina State Archives

By Steve Stolpen

Design by

Michael Brewer

Donning Company/Publishers
253 West Bute Street
Norfolk, Virginia 23510

A look at Fayetteville Street when both the trolley and the horse and carriage provided means for transportation. Dughi's was famous for its fresh homemade ice cream.

Courtesy of the Raleigh News and Observer

Raleigh

A Pictorial History

to my parents

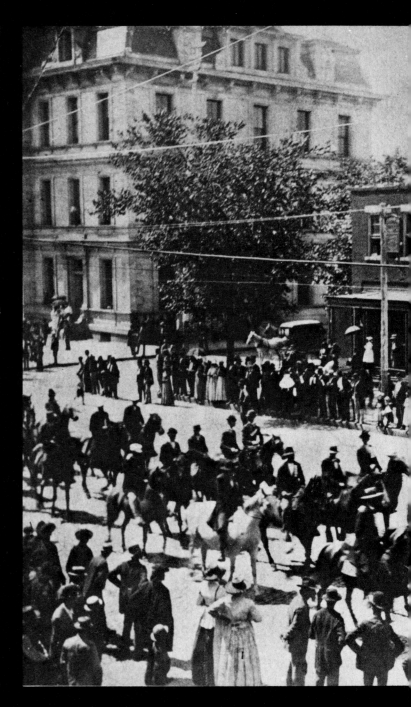

Library of Congress Cataloging in Publication Data

Stolpen, Steve, 1951-
Raleigh: a pictorial history.
1. Raleigh, N.C.—History—Pictorial works.
2. Raleigh, N.C.—Description—Views. I. Title.
F264.R1S75   975.6'55   77-1076
ISBN 0-915442-25-6

Printed in the United States of America

1892 was the year of Raleigh's Centennial Celebration.
One hundred years had passed since the founding of
the city. In this photograph, the Centennial parade
makes its way down Fayetteville Street. As you can
see, everyone in this photograph is wearing a head
covering. In those times, when one walked along
Fayetteville Street, one was sure to be properly
dressed. Men were expected to wear hats, women to
wear hats and gloves.

Courtesy of North Carolina State Archives

ACKNOWLEDGEMENTS

In drawing this book together, I received the help of so many persons that any list of acknowledgements would be incomplete. I would like to give thanks to Dr. Sarah Lemmon, who put her wide knowledge of history at my disposal, to Dick Langford and Ed Morris at the North Carolina State Archives, the staff of the North Carolina Collection, the Duke University Manuscript Department, and the photograph department of the Raleigh newspapers, to Mary V. Lassiter, to Maurice Toler of the North Carolina State University Archives, to Kenlon H. Brockwell and Tony Le May, to J. M. Crutchfield, David Boney, Hardy Berry, Emily Dickinson, Dianne D. Davis, H. K. Witherspoon, and the late photographer Albert Barden, who donated his vast collection of pictures to the State of North Carolina, from which many, many of the photographs in this book were gathered.

I would also like to acknowledge the help provided by several books including *North Carolina's Capital, Raleigh* by Elizabeth Waugh and an editorial committee, *The History of Wake County* by Hope Summerhill Chamberlain, *Raleigh, Capital of North Carolina* by the Writer's Program of the Work Projects Administration in the State of North Carolina, and *Raleigh, The Early Years* by Elizabeth Reid, "An Example of the New South?" by Dr. Sarah Lemmon in the *North Carolina Historical Review*, and "Raleigh Illustrated," a 1910 publication of the Raleigh Chamber of Commerce.

Final thanks go to Jim Baucam, and photographers Terry Cantrell, Jackson Hill, and Todd Huvard.

PENITENTIARY

REFERENCES

State Institutions.
Capitol
Insane Asylum
Penitentiary
Deaf and Dumb Asylum
(Colored)
Fair Grounds
Governor's Mansion
Public Buildings
Court House
Market House

Churches
Episcopal
Presbyterian
Methodist
Baptist
St. Paul
Methodist Chapel
Colored Episcopal
Colored Baptist
Colored Baptist

Miscellaneous

BIRD'S EYE VIEW OF THE CITY OF

RALEIGH

NORTH CAROLINA

INTRODUCTION

As one of the nation's original thirteen states, North Carolina has a history basic to a view of our country, and as Raleigh is the state's capital city, its history takes an important place in the context of a much larger scheme. But, Raleigh also has a past that is distinctly its own, and one that is of most interest to those who know her familiarly. It is for these people, the people of Raleigh, that this book has been composed. Though the book is in fact an historical rendering, its purpose is not so much an attempt to enlighten the student as it is to involve the interested. A photograph captures a moment in time. Raleigh is a city that is made rich by its past, and history itself is a study through time. These are readily joined to form a pictorial history of the city of Raleigh.

By no means has it been presumed to tell all that has happened in this city. In many instances, the choice of which facts to present depended on the particular photographs available, and as there clearly is not a photograph to lend itself to the telling of every significant moment, this account will not present all that could possibly be related. Still, much of what is central to the story of Raleigh can be found within these pages, and of course, the intention has also been to present the amusing and the interesting, along with the significant. The photographs included here show the city of Raleigh at various times in its past, showing the city streets, famous landmarks, influential citizens, and it is hoped that all the photographs will show something of the changes and similarities in the city's life when viewed over the span of years. It should also be mentioned that though considerable effort was made to insure the accuracy of the included statements, certain particular facts were gleaned from old clippings, conversations, and other more casual sources, and in such cases there were few means, if any, with which to verify these facts. Yet, such statements as these may still be correct.

In all, it took the help of many persons to gather the material in this book, and because so many in Raleigh are concerned with their history, quite a bit of information was made readily available. I would certainly like to thank all those who lent me photographs, information, and their help. It is hoped that on reading this book, one will not involve himself as a student of history, but rather as an observer of history. Even an old photograph presents a certain immediacy. In whiling away an hour, the reader may find himself far removed in time.

Steve Stolpen
Raleigh, 1977

This building is believed to have been Isaac Hunter's
tavern. If it is not the tavern itself, then it is one of
the outbuildings which stood nearby. A stipulation
was made by the North Carolina Assembly that the
Capital be located within ten miles of Hunter's
Tavern, which stood upon the stagecoach road
between Fayetteville and Petersburg at a distance of
about four miles to the north of the eventual location
of Union Square. This site would be near the present
day joining of New Hope Church Road and Wake
Forest Road. The building in the photograph was
moved a few hundred yards to the west of its original
site about 1920.

Courtesy of North Carolina State Archives

This land is thought to have held Isaac Hunter's
tavern.

Courtesy of North Carolina State Archives

BEGINNINGS

The origins of the Capital City of North Carolina are unlike those of most cities, which grow rather haphazardly, without plan or intention. A few settlers may gather in one spot, others may follow, and after a time, when the population of this place has grown, it may come to be known as a city. But Raleigh did not grow gradually; its development was not haphazard. Raleigh was planned from the very beginning, and in fact was so well planned that its original scheme is still very much intact as the heart of the city today. It has been said before; the city of Raleigh was born.

In colonial times, in 1771, the County of Wake was created from parts of Johnston, Cumberland, and Orange Counties by order of Royal Governor William Tryon. He is said to have chosen the county name for his wife Margaret Wake, though there are those who contend that this county was named for Esther Wake, the sister of Lady Tryon. In either case, the new county was a largely unsettled section in the heart of the colony. There were plantations, but the county could not boast of an important city.

During the revolutionary war, there was no one established center for the North Carolina government; the General Assembly convened in widely scattered places, such as Salem, Smithfield, Hillsborough, Halifax, and New Bern. One session of the General Assembly was held at a Wake County site which was sometimes called Bloomsbury, for it stood upon a hill within the estate of Joel Lane, and this estate had that name. With traveling conditions as arduous as they were in those times, legislators were often unable to attend meetings of the Assembly. One session, in 1780, never attained a quorum with the result that none of the issues of the day could be properly considered. After the war, North Carolina still had not fixed a permanent seat of government, and members of the General Assembly traveled to such towns as New Bern, Fayetteville, Hillsborough and Tarborough. It is reported in the WPA book that as early as 1779, an attempt was made to establish a government seat in either Johnston, Chatham, or Wake Counties, but the motion failed. In 1784 another proposal was rescinded which attempted to establish the Assembly in any of seven suggested sites, one of which was in Wake County.

The problem of locating a seat of government would persist until 1792. It was in 1781 that the Assembly finally passed a recommendation to establish one locale "for holding the future meetings of the General Assembly and the place of residence of the Chief officers of the state, which, when fixed, shall be considered the unalterable seat of government of this State." The following year, at the meeting of the Assembly in Hillsborough, an ordinance was made of the proposal of James Iredell to locate the Assembly in Wake County within ten miles of Isaac Hunter's tavern.

But there were certainly those who wished to have the Capital established in their own cities. Wilmington, Fayetteville, Hillsborough, Tarborough, and New Bern all vied to hold the seat of government, and their delegates pointed to the problems and expense of building a new city and to the disadvantages of locating the State Capital "in a place unconnected with commerce." The WPA book reports that at the Assembly of 1788 a petition signed by 119 delegates declaimed the choice of the Wake County site, and this delayed the eventual establishment of the Capital City of North Carolina. But by 1791, various competing claims for selection as the Capital had weakened, for no one city could gain the support of the others. In the end, delegates from Wilmington, the Albemarle, and the West threw in their lot with the proponents of the Wake County site, and the issue was settled.

It had been decided to locate the Capital within ten miles of Isaac Hunter's tavern, but the problem of exact selection of a site in this area was left to a group of Commissioners. These Commissioners were instructed by the Assembly to select a tract no less than six hundred acres and no more than one thousand. This area would hold a town of boundaries enclosing no less than four hundred acres. The Commissioners first met on the Hunter estate, but they soon moved to the Joel Lane home, where they debated the advantages of three tracts, that of Colonel John Hinton beyond the Neuse River near Milburnie, that of Nathaniel Jones near Cary, and the tract of land offered by Joel Lane.

After staying at Lane's home, the Commissioners agreed upon his tract. There have been those who have maintained that Joel Lane's punch, and whatever it was he may have added to it, has had a definite effect upon the flow of North Carolina history. The price of the land was set at thirty shillings per acre of "wooded and fresh ground," and the old-field was sold at a price of twenty shillings per acre. For a total sum equivalent to 2,756 dollars, a one-thousand acre tract was bought by the state to hold its Capital City, Raleigh.

Senator William Christmas was commissioned by the Assembly to draw the plan of the city. For a nominal fee, Christmas marked off a four hundred acre tract within the Lane purchase and laid out the system of streets and squares that still forms the heart of the city today. He was instructed to plan the city's

Perhaps today this fine home would not attract a great deal of attention. But in its time, Wakefield was noted as a "fine specimen of architectural elegance." Colonel Joel Lane's home is estimated to have been built either in 1760 or in one of the years immediately following that date. It now stands on Hargett Street as the oldest house in the city.

Lane may be aptly described as one of Raleigh's first and foremost citizens. He shared in laying the boundaries of Wake County and the streets of the Capital City. His tavern, in 1781, served as the meeting place for North Carolina's General Assembly. Lane was a Colonel in the Revolutionary Army, an Associate Justice for Wake County, a state senator through eleven sessions of the Assembly, and was one of the first trustees of the University of North Carolina. In addition, Lane was a planter and a speculator in real estate. For a price of 2,756 dollars paid in the year 1792, Joel Lane sold one thousand acres of land to the State of North Carolina, and it was upon this land that the city of Raleigh was established.

Photo by Jackson Hill

The interior of the Joel Lane House, photographed in the 1940s. The house had been closed, but was re-opened in the spring of 1976 by the Wake County Committee of the Colonial Dames of the State of North Carolina.

Courtesy of North Carolina State Archives

major streets to be ninety-nine feet wide and the others to be sixty-six feet wide. His plan included the division of the tract into lots designated for private and governmental proprietorship. Sale of these lots was accomplished by an auction held in June of 1792, and of the 254 lots offered to the public, 212 were bought at the auction. A city had been marked off in the wilderness of central North Carolina in accord with a plan which envisioned and accommodated coming growth and grandeur. It would be the 1850s before the city limits were extended one-fourth mile in each direction beyond the original boundaries of the Christmas plan.

Still, the early growth of the Capital City was slow and uncertain. There were very few who were enticed to take up residence in the new city "of streets without houses," and it even required an official act to have the State Governor make his permanent residence in the city. In 1800 the population was counted at a mere 669 persons. In its first years, Raleigh was little more than an isolated small town, but one accustomed to the passing of leading individuals of the day, and one in which the fabric of daily life would be interwoven with the affairs of the state.

In her *History of Wake County,* Hope Summerhill Chamberlain quotes Colonel Creecy's *Grandfather's Tales* to present a picture of Raleigh at the beginning of the nineteenth century: "It was a town of magnificent distances, of unsightly bramble bush, and briers, of hills and morasses, of grand old oaks and few inhabitants, and an 'onwelcome' look to newcomers." On Union Square there still stood a sassafras tree which marked the place where a hunter had once positioned himself to shoot forty deer in a single day. The cattle were left free to roam the woods, and some say that herds of pigs would graze on Union Square. This last practice probably was put to an end with the erection of the first monument on Capitol grounds, which was Hubard's bronze replica of Houdon's marble statue of George Washington. Some reports say that the iron fence which used to surround Capitol Square, and which now encloses the City Cemetery, was originally placed about the Square to keep out the farm animals that paraded freely along the town's streets. In all, these statements about Raleigh's earliest years provide a picture of a very different town than we know today, and show that though Raleigh was destined from its birth to take an important place in the affairs of North Carolina, its very beginnings were those of a small country town. Decades later a visitor to Raleigh would remark, somewhat disdainfully, that the most prevalent architectural form within the city was "still the log-cabin."

In the first decades of the nineteenth century the primary crops, and often the only crops, were wheat and corn. The stores on Fayetteville Street sold only the staple goods; the extravagant articles which could be found in older communities were not to be bought in the shops of Raleigh. The education of children was primarily the concern of the home. The idea of free and compulsory education was well beyond the ken of most of the city's inhabitants, though the Raleigh Academy was established in the early 1800s on Burke Square to provide classes for some of the city's children. Hope Chamberlain describes as one of Raleigh's first educators a Negro named John Chavis, who was a slave and who was sent to Princeton to be educated as a Presbyterian minister. This was purportedly done as an experiment to determine how much a black man could learn. When Chavis returned after completing his work at Princeton, he found himself in the unique position of being a black man who had been educated as a minister. He could not be put back with the slaves and he could not be accepted as an equal by the white citizens. It has been reported that when John Chavis dined, he would be seated in the same room with the white people, but that he ate at a separate table, and that this custom came to be generally used to resolve one of the social perplexities arising in the case of the black minister John Chavis. After his return to Raleigh, Chavis taught classes for white children during the day and classes for black children at night, and in later years he taught the children of prominent families throughout the state.

The young country town of Raleigh, perhaps not having yet attained the dignity that befitted a capital city, could still boast of at least three hotels. There were The Eagle, and The Indian Queen, and Peter Casso's Inn which stood at the corner of Morgan and Fayetteville Streets. It was at Peter Casso's that the stage would stop, having come from the north to travel on to Fayetteville. The arrival of the stage was a glad event in the weekly life of the city, for with the stage came travelers and news. Chamberlain relates that the townspeople would greet the stage at Casso's and listen to the stories of the travelers, receive the mail, and read the newspapers of faraway cities with their reports of cities and countries even more distant. The stage was the town's link with the outside world.

One event may be looked back upon as signaling the beginning of change in the nature of the country town of Raleigh. In 1831, the old State House on Union Square was destroyed by fire. This calamity nearly caused Raleigh to lose the honor of holding the state seat of government. Those in Fayetteville, still wishing their city to become the State Capital, began to clamor that the government center might well be moved as the construction of a new State House was

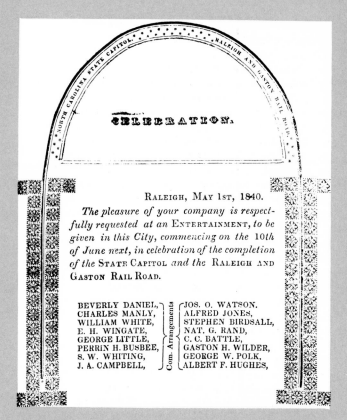

An invitation to the celebration for the completion of
the Capitol and the Raleigh and Gaston Railroad.
Dinners were served, tours were conducted through the
new Capitol, and at night this building was the scene
of a grand ball. Elizabeth Reid's "Raleigh, The Early
Years," mentions that Weston R. Gales, one of the
city's editors, gave a toast at an afternoon dinner
and said that Raleigh had "exceeded in gallantry even
its own renowned namesake, Sir Walter. He but laid
down his cloak for one lady to walk over. Its citizens
have helped to lay down eighty-six miles of Rail Road
for the whole sex to ride over."

Courtesy of North Carolina State Archives

now required. For a time it seemed that North Carolina's "unalterable" seat of government would be relocated. Supposedly, there was even talk of establishing a new city, called Haywood, as the State Capital. In the face of this opposition, Henry Seawell in the Senate and William Henry Haywood, Jr. in the House of Commons made the respective motions to rebuild a Capitol on Union Square in Raleigh. Legislators throughout the state were undecided on which course to take, and it has been said it was the matchless eloquence of William Gaston that finally persuaded the wavering officials to vote to maintain the Capital in Raleigh. Funds were allocated, and the magnificent new capitol was completed in 1840.

One other occurrence, coinciding with the completion of the Capitol, would signify the beginning of a new stage in the development of the city of Raleigh, and that was the coming of the railroad. This new means of transportation had already linked many other cities, and the people of Raleigh began to demand the railroad and the advantages it would bring. In 1840 a train pulled by the locomotive *Tornado* accomplished the eighty-six mile trip from Gaston to become the first ever to arrive in Raleigh. With the completion of the railroad and the new Capitol, the city held three days of celebration.

The railroad heralded an era of increased prosperity, and such prosperity brought growth. More goods could be transported more easily, and the results were extremely favorable in the pre-Civil War agricultural South. Grocers in Raleigh, who had previously only sold staple goods, began to attract more shoppers with shelves holding syrups and candies and raisins and figs. Clothing styles became generally more extravagant, as milliners sold trimmed bonnets and dresses with leg-o-mutton sleeves. The men might be seen wearing tailor-made tight blue tailcoats with brass buttons and high velvet collars, and cravats wound twice about the neck and holding up the pointed collars of white shirts. In many ways, the good life had come to Raleigh.

This era of prosperity was short-lived, lasting little more than two decades, for it preceded the great American Civil War. No one could ever speak more aptly of the passing of those pre-war times than did Margaret Mitchell when she wrote of them as having "gone with the wind." In the state of North Carolina as a whole, there was at first relatively little wish to secede, but as the political rifts deepened, opposing factions developed within the state, as they did within Raleigh. Chamberlain reports that in 1861, on Fayetteville Street, after the firing at Fort Sumter, secessionists mounted red cockades and a flag reflecting their sentiments. The unionists fired at the flag and the secessionists fired back at the unionists. No one was injured. Governor Ellis then made his way to the scene of the quarrel, when, it is said, he was handed the telegram which announced Lincoln's call for troops from North Carolina. Few, if any, would fight on the side of the North, and the question of secession had been settled.

Raleigh, herself, was fortunate in that the battles which were fought in the course of the war were not staged in her vicinity. Early in the war it had been decided by a board of surgeons that the city's splendid climate would have a salubrious effect upon the sick and wounded, and Raleigh was designated as a site for Confederate military hospitals. In this capacity and as a supply depot, Raleigh took her part in Confederate military operations, and she was spared the ravaging and destruction that brought the ruin of other towns. But though Raleigh herself escaped the war's desolation, her citizens underwent the hardships and privations, the bereavements and heartbreak that come to a people at war. An era of good feeling had been abruptly ended by the onset of national catastrophe, and for the South, the wounds she often suffered could hardly be survived.

As the war approached its close, and as the Union forces chased the fleeing Confederates through North Carolina, the city of Raleigh began the construction of fortifications about her perimeter, but fortunately, these defenses were never necessary and were never used. With the war all but over, the city agreed to surrender to General Judson Kilpatrick, who led an advance column of Union soldiers. Kilpatrick relayed this news to General Sherman, who sent back his promises of protection for Confederate officials and for the protection of the property of the city's inhabitants as long as no hostile acts were committed against the oncoming Union Army. These promised protections were very nearly lost, when, as the Federal forces camped upon Fayetteville Street, one young Confederate soldier rode up to and fired upon a column of Union troops. The soldier then turned and attempted to flee upon his horse, but he was quickly overtaken and captured. Soon, he was hanged. With the exception of this incident, the city's surrender was accomplished peacefully, and the words of David Lowry Swain, which have been recorded in Hope Summerhill Chamberlain's *History of Wake County,* recount the closing of the war in Raleigh: "About three o'clock in the afternoon, in company with Governor Graham, who had risked life and reputation on behalf of this community to an extent of which those who derived the advantage are little aware, I delivered the keys of the State House to General Sherman at the gubernatorial mansion...."

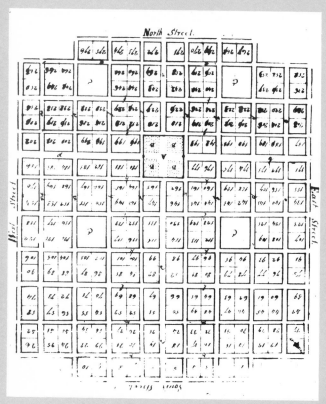

In accord with this plan, drawn by William Christmas in 1792, the city of Raleigh was built. As provided for from the very first, Raleigh has been graced with a neat and logical system of streets and squares. William Christmas served the state as surveyor in the planning of the Capital, and for his work in laying out the city of Raleigh, he received a fee of one hundred and ten dollars. The original tract of land encompassed by the Christmas plan consisted of only four hundred acres. Still, the city would not expand beyond its first boundaries for more than half a century.

Courtesy of the North Carolina Collection

Here, drawn in 1797, is a more detailed plan for the city. Fayetteville, Hillsborough, Salisbury, New Bern, Edenton, Halifax, Morgan, and Wilmington Streets were named for the state's judicial districts. This naming may well have been done to appease those North Carolinians whose cities weren't chosen as the State Capital. Streets were also named for prominent North Carolinians, Stephen Cabarrus, William Lenoir, William Richardson Davie, and for Joel Lane, upon whose land the city was built. Other streets were named for Commissioners Blount, McDowell, Harrington, Dawson, Jones, Person, Martin, and Hargett. Six acre Union Square was placed near the center of the city, and the other four squares, of four acres each, were named for governors Burke, Nash, and Caswell, and for the state's first Attorney General, Moore.

Courtesy of the North Carolina Collection

NEW BEGINNINGS

As every end is a beginning, and as the Civil War and its close marked the end of a distinct cultural era in the South, it also heralded new times of growth and enterprise for the nation as a whole, and the city of Raleigh would join in the bustle of those times. But this era would not commence without the necessary attention to post-war problems and rebuilding, and without the confusing infringements of imposed reconstruction. The agriculturally based economic system of the South had run down in the course of the war, and one of its main supports had crumbled with the abolition of slavery. Then, too, the West had begun to throw its weight into the national economic balance, and the South would be slow to regain its former standing. These times were especially frustrating to the people of the southern states; it was difficult to comprehend that a system and an attendant way of life had become a part of the past and could no longer constitute a viable part of the inter-workings of the modern day. The South would have to wait until the form of a new era had made itself apparent.

Since the days before the War for Independence, a spirit of optimism ran through this country, and part of that optimism was the assurance that one day this American nation would take its place among the great powers of the world. From the time of the close of the Civil War and the following years of rebuilding, and until the time of the first World War, there was little to mar that national assurance; often standing apart from international affairs, the United States was left alone to expand, solidify itself and develop, and the events and texture of this era formed a national welding of sentiment and accomplishment that we Americans have assumed as part of our national character up until the very present day.

It has always been a benefit to the city of Raleigh to have been the planned Capital City of North Carolina. If the United States had previously been known as a land of individualism, of wilderness, and of simplistic values, in the latter decades of the nineteenth century, she would turn inward in seeking growth and maturity. Raleigh, with a neat layout of streets and squares, was inherently prepared to establish its own distinctiveness and character, without undergoing the problems of organization that beset many another expanding city. The age of industry had simply come of age, and with the opportunities it brought arose the demands for new enterprises, for public education, for progress and modernization.

In 1880, Raleigh's population was counted at little more than nine thousand persons. According to WPA records, in that decade the city could boast of three tobacco warehouses, two boiler factories, three foundries, four carriage and wagon factories, and four planing mills. This list shows that Raleigh could hardly be counted among the great industrial complexes, but that her leaders were beginning to seek growth along the lines of the new opportunities offered by the day. By the time of World War I, at the end of this forward-moving era, Raleigh could claim sixty-seven manufacturing plants. Within this time had come a city water system, telephone systems, organized fire departments, cotton mills, the foundations of a public school system, and hospitals.

In this era bent on mechanized progress and change, one would be neglectful not to mention the vagaries of individual influences. Raleigh, in the time of the advancing eighties, did only have one locksmith, whose name was Thomas Francisco Brockwell. The vocation in those days was given the title of safecracker. Somehow it happened that the vault in Raleigh's largest bank became locked and could not be opened. The bank president called in the safecracker, Thomas Francisco Brockwell. Brockwell soon had the safe open, and the bank president reached into a leather change purse he had tied about his waist, produced a quarter, a dime, and two nickels, and asked how much he owed. Brockwell didn't feel he was owed very much when he slammed the vault door back shut and left. Another safecracker was soon called in from out of town, and before going to the bank, he stopped at Brockwell's shop, where a certain professional rapport developed. After arriving at the bank, it took the out of town expert several days to open the vault, while the city's commerce slowed and all but stopped. This, when Brockwell had already given the lock combination to the other safecracker. It is said that in later years, differences between the bank president and the safecracker were eventually forgotten, and that Brockwell made a present to the banker of a gold-handled cane.

It can be gathered that though Raleigh may have changed with the nature of the era, she could hardly be described as having been transformed. As always, Raleigh was a Capital City, designed to serve the needs of a government center rather than an industrial complex. In those days Raleigh's reputation as a "fashionable" town grew considerably. Victorian homes, that were widely admired, were added to the city streets. In time, the city became the home of several schools. Saint Mary's had been formed before the Civil War and there was Peace Institute, planned before the war, but which did not hold classes until well after the war had ended. The city's two black schools, Saint Augustine's and Shaw, were formed

A 1930s aerial view of downtown Raleigh.
Courtesy of North Carolina State Archives

during the early post-war years. A and M, which has become North Carolina State University, was created in 1887, and Meredith College was chartered in 1891. These, and the presence of prestigious public buildings and homes styled in earlier eras formed the civic character, and Raleigh was then as now, a blend of the old and new.

Much of the Raleigh that is known today grew in the years after the first world war, and in many cases, it will be the people in Raleigh who grew up in those years who may have their recollections matched by the photographs in this book. As it happened, the greatest number of the photographs gathered were taken in the years between 1890 and about 1920. One reason was that the art of photography itself had developed to a point by 1890 that many more persons than ever before could take clear and pleasing pictures. This clarity, and the distance that separates us from those times, seemed to make the photographs of this era the most likely and interesting to be preserved in this collection. This was the era that could best be examined pictorially by the generations which followed its passing.

The Writer's Program of the Work Projects Administration wrote a history of Raleigh on the occasion of the city's sesquicentennial anniversary in 1942. An amusing comment which appeared in that history will be repeated here; they quoted a columnist who wrote that in 1920, "Chivalry made its last stand when the North Carolina General Assembly, in special session, made an heroic effort to protect Southern womanhood from the dangers of the ballot." The era we know today would seem to have had its beginning in the times after World War I. For this period, there are probably as many historians as there are people wishing to tell the tale, and this account would not seem to hold a place for speaking too generally of times so many Raleigh citizens have known personally and that have been colored in the recollection by the nature of individual experiences. But, these were the times in which Raleigh cast off all vestiges of the appearance of a small town and in which it grew to become the substantial city it is today. For these times, it is hoped that the photographs collected will serve to sharpen and intrigue the memories of those who have known them and to stimulate the interest of those who will know them only from books such as this.

The city of Raleigh is anchored by monument and the principles of what has gone before. Most obviously, and perhaps most emphatically, Raleigh is shaped today, as it was designed nearly two hundred years ago, in accord with a plan for a Capital City

that has survived, for the most part, through that time. Still, in the plan for the immediate future is at least one notable change in the city's basic scheme. That, of course, is the transition of Fayetteville Street into the Downtown Mall in order to restore the vitality of the city's central core. With the mall will come a new Civic Center, and the city's essential shape will have undergone substantial change. Raleigh shares in the seemingly universal problems of expansion and direction that trouble most every sizable metropolis in the country, and one of her proposed solutions is to turn attention back inward to the city core. It is apparent that Raleigh, the planned Capital, will only undergo change through further planning, and all such planning will necessarily hinge upon the strictures of design which formed the city in 1792.

Of great concern to the Capital City in its future will be the preservation of its historic landmarks, for the past of this city has created much of its present distinguished character. In recent years, the Mordecai Historic Park has been established, and within this park, the Mordecai House, the Andrew Johnson birthplace, the Allen kitchen, and the tiny temple-like building which likely served as Raleigh's first Post Office have all been preserved. The Historic Properties Commission has designated forty points within the city as Raleigh landmarks. In addition, the Oakwood section of town had been designated as an historic district, and now this same designation is applied to Capitol Square and to North Blount Street. These steps in the preservation of historic Raleigh should lead to others. To maintain the character of this city, the future will necessarily be concerned with the city's past.

For now, and for this part of our history, quite enough has been said. Enclosed in these pages are many photographs, representing captured moments in time, which will show more than can be said with words of Raleigh's history. Let's take a look at that history, moment by moment.

Sir Walter Raleigh was born in East Budleigh near Exmouth, Devan. The people of this part of England were a seafaring lot, and of course, Sir Walter was no exception.

Courtesy of North Carolina State Archives

The famed Englishman, Sir Walter Raleigh. The gallantry of this gentleman was well-remembered in an idealistic young nation that had only recently won its independence from one of the mightiest world powers. This, coupled with the fact that he had attempted to establish an English Colony at Manteo off the North Carolina coast, made his name a likely and popular choice for the Capital City of North Carolina. Interestingly enough, Sir Walter, who never visited his namesake city, spelled his own last name Ralegh.

Courtesy of North Carolina State Archives

Mr. Willie Jones, of Halifax, did much to bring about the selection of the Wake County site as the Capital of North Carolina. Just why he favored this site is now uncertain, but records indicate that he used his considerable political skills to persuade members of the Assembly to vote for the Wake County location. Eventually, Jones moved to the Raleigh vicinity and built a home named "Welcome Place" where, aptly enough, he received many distinguished visitors.

Courtesy of North Carolina State Archives

The Mordecai House was built about 1785 as a wedding present from Joel Lane to his son Henry and his bride Mary (Polly) Hinton Lane. Originally, the house consisted of three rooms and one and a half stories. It was enlarged over the years, and the photo shows the home as it has been preserved at the Mordecai Historic Park. It is a fine example of Greek Revival architecture, employing both Ionic and Doric columns.

The house takes its name from its second owner, the astute lawyer, Moses Mordecai. Mordecai married twice into the Lane family. He first married Margaret Lane. Upon her death, he wed her sister, Ann.

Courtesy of the Division of Travel and Promotion
Photo by Clay Nolen

Elmwood still stands in Raleigh at 16 North Boylan Avenue, and it is still privately owned. It was built on a five acre plot by the first Chief Justice of the State Supreme Court, John Louis Taylor. It would later serve as the home of William Gaston, who was a Supreme Court Justice, Thomas Ruffin, who was another Supreme Court Chief Justice, and Romulus M. Saunders, and noted North Carolina historian and editor Samual A'Court Ashe. Two of his daughters own and live in Elmwood today.

Originally, the front yard extended seventy yards to Hillsborough Street; a service station is now on the front part of the property. In this photo, taken shortly before 1870, members and servants of the Saunders family are seen standing before the house.

Courtesy of North Carolina State Archives

Elmwood, an interior view from the 1940s.

Courtesy of North Carolina State Archives

The White-Holman-McCanless House of 209 East Morgan Street was built by William White, Secretary of State from 1798 to 1810. It exemplifies the style of row houses that were popular in France and England in the early seventeenth century. Such houses were arranged in rows about the public squares, and this design conserved space. Of course, the architectural styling of this house did not need to have this purpose in early Raleigh.

Courtesy of North Carolina State Archives

The Crabtree Jones House was named for its original owner, whose real name, by the way, was Nathaniel Jones. Records show that there were three Jones' of that name in the county. There were Nathaniel Jones, Sr., Nathaniel of Crabtree, and Nathaniel of White Plains. To avoid confusion, the habit developed of calling one of these men White Plains Jones and the other Crabtree Jones. The Nathaniel Jones who built this house served in the state assembly between 1777 and 1818. The Crabtree Jones house is an excellent example of an early Southern American farmhouse, displaying molded weatherboarding, molded window sills, and detailed window and door casings.

Courtesy of North Carolina State Archives

The Cameron House was built by Judge Duncan
Cameron as his second home in 1835. Cameron removed
to Raleigh from his gigantic estate, Fairntosh, and
built this home off Hillsborough Street. During his
time in Raleigh, Judge Cameron chaired the committee
which was responsible for the building of the second
Capitol, and he was in charge of the building of Christ
Church. Cameron was also president of the North
Carolina State Bank. The Cameron House was taken
down in 1938, the land was subdivided many times,
and part of the original estate now holds Cameron
Village.

Courtesy of North Carolina State Archives

Haywood Hall of 211 New Bern Avenue was built by
John Haywood. Haywood was born in Edgecombe
County and came to Raleigh in 1792 after having been
unanimously elected State Treasurer by the General
Assembly. He also became Raleigh's first Intendant of
Police, or mayor. Haywood Hall is still used as a
private residence today. The drawing was made by
Edwin Hodgkins.

Courtesy of North Carolina State Archives

The Cosby-Heartt House stood at the corner of
Hargett and Dawson Streets. The original part of the
house was of federal styling. Dabney Cosby, a Raleigh
architect, bought the house about 1830, and added the
section shown in this photograph. The house was
taken down in the early 1950s.

Courtesy of North Carolina State Archives
Photo by North Carolina W.P.A. Art Project

EAGLE HOTEL,

AND STAGE-OFFICE,
RALEIGH, N. C.
CHARLES PARISH

INFORMS his Friends and the Public that his Tavern is now open for the reception of Travellers and Boarders in the new Three Story Brick-House, north of the State-House and fronting Union Square. The house is spacious, completely finished, and well furnished; and the Stables are equal to any. For a well supplied Table, (served from a neat and cleanly Kitchen,) luxuries of the Cellar, Rooms, Beds, Attendance, &c. &c. it is determined that this Tavern shall excel any in the Southern States.

Raleigh, July 1, 1812.

N. B An Ice House and Bathing Rooms will be constructed by the next Season.

The Northern Stage arrives at this Tavern every other day to dinner.

Early in the nineteenth century, two Raleigh hotels advertise for patronage.

Courtesy of the North Carolina Collection

WILLIAM SCOTT's TAVERN,

AT THE SIGN OF THE
INDIAN QUEEN,
NEAR THE COURT-HOUSE
RALEIGH,

HAS lately been greatly improved by the addition of Dining Room, forty four feet long, and several convenient apartments for private accommodation. The Larder and Cellar are and constantly will be well stored with every thing that can contribute to the comfort of the Traveller. The rooms are well furnished, have clean beds, and will be well attended. The stables are spacious, contain a variety of forage and provender, are attended by faithful hostlers, and has a carriage house annexed.—— The News-papers of all the principal towns in the United States are regularly received and kept on file in the Public Room. Every exertion will be made to please. The patronage of the public is respectfully solicited, and all favours will be gratefully acknowledged.

Raleigh, September 6, 1810.

This bell, which is in the possession of the North Carolina Museum of History, has the words "Raleigh Courthouse" inscribed on its side. The inscription is curious, for the bell, cast in 1804, would have been used at the Wake County Courthouse. which was erected in 1795 at the present Courthouse site, on land donated by Theophilus Hunter and Thomas Bloodworth. There was no "Raleigh" courthouse at this time, and perhaps the fact that the bell was cast in faraway Philadelphia accounts for the mistaken inscription.

Courtesy of North Carolina State Archives

This silver medal was awarded at the first State Fair, held in 1853 on a site approximately ten blocks east of the Capitol, about where the Motor Vehicle Building now stands.

Courtesy of North Carolina State Archives

The law office of William Gaston stood on the southwest corner of Salisbury and West Hargett Streets. A native of New Bern, Gaston was highly regarded in Raleigh as a man of broad intelligence and capability. He was also considered to be one of the foremost orators of the time. From 1800 to 1832 he served four terms in the State Senate and seven in the House of Commons, and he was a member of the United States House of Representatives from 1813 until 1817. Gaston was a North Carolina Supreme Court Justice from 1833 until 1844.

Courtesy of North Carolina State Archives

It was written in the state constitution that no Roman Catholic could hold public office, but in the case of the esteemed William Gaston, this stricture was overlooked. Gaston also was among the tiny minority in his time to oppose slavery, and his judicial decisions clearly reflected his determination to protect the civil rights of slaves. His opinions upon this issue would have made many enemies for a lesser individual, but Gaston was well-liked and widely respected in the community. Gaston authored the official North Carolina song, "The Old North State."

Courtesy of North Carolina State Archives

North Carolina's first State House was built upon
Union Square, between 1792 and 1794. Originally, it
was a plain two-story building, but an eastern wing, a
domed rotunda, and a western wing were added in the
early 1820s. This painting by Jacob Marling shows the
State House with these later additions. For many years
religious services were held in the State House. It was
lost to fire in 1831.

Courtesy of North Carolina State Archives

GEORGE
WASHINGTON
1732 — 1799

ANTONIO CANOVA
1757 — 1822

The Canova Statue

In its time the original statue of George Washington, by Antonio Canova, was considered to be the most sublime work of art in the United States. In 1815 a bill was passed by the State Assembly calling for the purchase of a statue of the American leader, and it was agreed that there would be no limit placed upon the sum the state would be willing to spend. Thomas Jefferson was consulted, and he opined that Antonio Canova, the renowned Italian sculptor, be commissioned. When approached, Canova, an admirer of the American patriot, quite willingly agreed to execute the statue. It was hewn from white marble and brought to Raleigh in November of 1821.

When the statue was placed in the State House, the people of Raleigh were astonished to see that Canova had depicted Washington clad in Roman toga and sandals. But in time these same people were able to appreciate the classical dignity Canova had lent to the figure, and they began to take immense pride in the statue on display in the rotunda of the State House. According to Chamberlain's *History of Wake County,* at some point it was suggested that the Canova statue be mounted on a wheeled platform so that it might be moved in the event of calamity. But to the people of that time, mounting the statue on wheels would lessen its dignity, and this precaution was never taken.

On June 21, 1831, a fire was started in the State House from a solder pot left upon the roof. The flames were spotted, but there was no way to extinguish them, and the people of Raleigh had no recourse but to stand by helplessly as the State House burned slowly. Miss Betsy Geddy called upon those who watched the fire to try to move the statue, but it was far too heavy to be budged. The people of Raleigh had to watch as the flames surrounded the statue. Chamberlain reports that they watched as it was heated and as it glowed with an unearthly red color, and they watched as the roof of the State House collapsed, smashing the statue.

Most fortunately, the Canova statue has not been lost. Early in the twentieth century the working model Canova had used was uncovered in Possagno, Italy, and the Italian government had a plaster of Paris copy made, which was given to North Carolina in 1910. In the 1960s, funds were raised to have a marble copy made of the Possagno model. The new marble statue was completed in 1970 and was placed in the rotunda of the Capitol.

Courtesy of North Carolina State Archives

The Capitol Building of the State of North Carolina
was built upon Union Square to replace the old State
House which burned in 1831. At the time of the
Capitol's completion, in 1840, it had cost 532,682
dollars, a sum more than three times greater than the
yearly income of the state.

The stone walls of the Capitol are formed of
gneiss, a type of granite which was quarried in
southeastern Raleigh. North Carolina's first railroad
system, which was really a tramway system, was used
in transporting the stone. Chamberlain reports that
young Leonidas Polk, who was later to become Bishop
Polk, was on a visit to Boston when he spied such
a system already in use. He wrote to his family,
describing the system, and included in his letter a
detailed drawing of the tramway. The Polks capitalized
on the idea, and Raleigh's Experimental Railroad
came to be. It consisted of little more than mules pulling
flat carts along a track. On Sundays it was fashionable
to take a ride on this, Raleigh's first "railway" system.

Courtesy of Duke University Manuscript Department

Courtesy of North Carolina State Archives

President Vass of the Raleigh and Gaston Railroad poses atop one of the company's locomotives. The year is 1850. In 1840 a railroad train rode this company's line from Gaston to become the first ever to arrive in Raleigh. The distance from Raleigh to Gaston was eighty-six miles, and round trip could be accomplished in twelve hours. For the first passengers, it was a giddy pace.

Courtesy of North Carolina State Archives

The "Raleigh," designed and constructed in England, was one of the early locomotives of the Raleigh-Gaston line.

Courtesy of North Carolina State Archives

In the year 1842, this following notice was placed
in newspapers throughout the south and the east: "The
Rev. Albert Smedes of the City of New York, designs
to open a School for Young Ladies in the City of
Raleigh, North Carolina, on the 12th day of May next.
This institution is to furnish a thorough and elegant
Education."

The school was St. Mary's. This photograph of
the school's chapel predates 1900. The chapel itself
was largely modeled on a drawing by Richard
Upjohn, the noted British architect who designed
Trinity Church in New York and Raleigh's Christ
Church.

Courtesy of North Carolina State Archives

Smedes Hall, on the Saint Mary's campus, was built
about 1835 and originally housed an Episcopal school
for boys. During the summer of 1863, Mrs. Jefferson
Davis and her children took refuge in Smedes Hall
when it was feared that Richmond would fall. Wings
were added to the building in 1909.

Courtesy of North Carolina State Archives

Credit for the building of the State Hospital for the Insane may be given to Dorothea Dix. Miss Dix did not allow the hospital to be named for herself. In 1847 she toured the state and decided that such a facility was desperately needed. She came to Raleigh in 1848 and persuaded members of the Democratic party to promote her cause. The first bill for the asylum was defeated.

Chamberlain's *History of Wake County* states that Miss Dix stayed in a hotel while in Raleigh, and in this same hotel were James Dobbin and his wife. In this time, Mrs. Dobbin contracted a fatal illness, and through the course of this illness she was attended by Miss Dix. Before she died, Mrs. Dobbin asked her husband to help Dorothea Dix in her fight for the hospital. After the funeral, James Dobbin spoke in behalf of the hospital before the Assembly. The emotional force of his appeal could not be denied. The hospital was built. Though Miss Dix would not have wished it for herself, the hospital is generally known today by her name.

Courtesy of North Carolina State Archives

Known as the Henry Clay Oak, this tree stands one hundred feet west of the northwest corner of North Blount and East North Streets. It is thought to be between three and five hundred years old, and it measures seventeen and one half feet in circumference. On a visit to Raleigh in March, 1844, Henry Clay stayed at the home of Congressman Kenneth Raynor. It is told that Clay reflected beneath the shade of this tree as he came to decide upon writing his famous letter opposing the annexation of Texas. He later defended his statements in this letter, saying, "I had rather be right than to be President." Clay's stand against the annexation of Texas, as much as anything else, made sure that he would indeed, not be President.

Courtesy of the North Carolina Collection

The Haywood House, built in 1854 by Dr. Richard B. Haywood, still serves as a private residence at 127 East Edenton Street. Bay windows at either side of the house were installed in accord with the wish of Dr. Haywood's wife, Julia Ogden Hicks.

Courtesy of North Carolina State Archives

Charles L. Hinton built Midway Plantation at a point between two other family plantations, "The Oaks" and "Beaver Dam." It was built for Hinton's son, Major David Hinton, and his bride, Mary Boddie Carr Hinton, at a distance of about eight miles east of the Capitol, and was completed in 1848.

The plantation lay in the path of the force of General John A. Logan as it made its way to Raleigh from the Battle of Bentonville in 1865. The property was vandalized, but the house itself was saved. Mrs. Hinton, before fleeing to Raleigh, buried the family's silver and sank a box of the family's gold pieces in the pond. Later, the pond was drained, and the gold was recovered.

Courtesy of North Carolina State Archives

Montfort Hall was built in the late 1850s by William Montfort Boylan, the playful son of a more sober and industrious millionaire father, William Boylan. In *North Carolina's Capital, Raleigh,* author Elizabeth Waugh says this about the mansion's owner: "He kept a fine stable, bred his own horses, rode to hounds, drank good whiskey, cursed eloquently, and represented all that went with inheriting an antebellum fortune in the South." Today, what was once the home of a hard-drinking millionaire is now the property of the Boylan Heights Baptist Church.

The Hogg-Dortch House was built in the 1850s on North Wilmington Street by Dr. Thomas Devereux Hogg. Union soldiers camped upon the grounds after the war. The house was taken down in 1962.

Courtesy of North Carolina State Archives

Since 1968, the State Library and Museum of History have been located in this building, which stands on the former grounds of the Hogg-Dortch estate.

Courtesy of North Carolina State Archives

The Lawrence O'Bryan Branch House was built about 1850. In his time, Branch was President of the Raleigh-Gaston Railroad, a Congressman, and a Confederate general during the Civil War. Branch fell at the Battle of Antietam in 1862.

Courtesy of North Carolina State Archives

Quite plainly demonstrating the elements of Greek Revival Architecture, the Lewis-Smith House was built on North Wilmington Street in the 1850s by Dr. Augustus Lewis. Lewis at one time was a member of the General Assembly, representing Wake County. Dr. Charles Lee Smith bought the residence in 1913.

Courtesy of North Carolina State Archives

The Tucker carriage house, as it may still be seen on St. Mary's Street.

It is told in the *History of Wake County* that the great wooden beaver which served as the shop sign for the hatter William Peck was stolen upon a Saturday evening. The thief was not identified until the following morning when he appeared at church service carrying the sign and wearing huge goggles, a top hat, an over-sized overcoat, and leaning upon a cane. The scoundrel was identified as young Rufus Sylvester Tucker.

Later in life, Tucker was to become one of Raleigh's most respected citizens. During the Civil War he would organize a company of cavalry. Eventually, he would direct the Raleigh National Bank and four railroad companies. Tucker took a large part in the affairs of the city of Raleigh, and he held several official positions. He also was one of the city's first historians. The house he built, in 1858, near the corner of St. Mary's and Hillsborough Streets, was considered to be one of Raleigh's most magnificent homes. Each of the two towers housed water tanks. The home has been torn down in this century.

Courtesy of North Carolina State Archives

Andrew Johnson, President of the United States after the Civil War, was born in this house. At the time of his birth, it stood on Fayetteville Street near Peter Casso's Inn, where his father worked as a hostler. The house was eventually moved to East Cabarrus Street, and then to one, and then another site in Pullen Park, and recently it has been moved again to the Mordecai Historic Park.

Courtesy of North Carolina State Archives

Ten Dollars Reward.

RAN AWAY from the Subscriber, on the night of the 15th instant, two apprentice boys, legally bound, named WILLIAM and ANDREW JOHNSON The former is of a dark complexion, black hair, eyes, and habits. They are much of a height, about 5 feet 4 or 5 inches The latter is very fleshy, freckled face, light hair, and fair complexion. They went off with two other apprentices, advertised by Messrs Wm. & Chas. Fowler When they went away, they were well clad—blue cloth coats, light colored homespun coats, and new hats, the maker's name in the crown of the hats, is Theodore Clark. I will pay the above Reward to any person who will deliver said apprentices to me in Raleigh, or I will give the above Reward for Andrew Johnson alone.

All persons are cautioned against harboring or employing said apprentices, on pain of being prosecuted.

JAMES J. SELBY, Tailor.
Raleigh, N.C. June 24, 1824   26 3t

On June 25, 1824, this reward notice for the return of runaway apprentices William and Andrew Johnson appeared in the *North Carolina Gazette* and *The Star*. In all likelihood, the future President's term of apprenticeship extended until he reached the age of twenty-one. Wanting his freedom, the sixteen year old Andrew Johnson fled from his apprenticeship in Raleigh to make his way in South Carolina.

Courtesy of North Carolina State Archives

During his term as president, in 1867, Johnson returned to Raleigh to attend the dedication of this city cemetery monument for his father, Jacob Johnson. The inscription calls Jacob Johnson "An honest man, beloved and respected by all who knew him," and it says that he died "from a disease caused by an over effort in saving the life of his friend." It was told that Jacob Johnson's health suffered and eventually failed after he had risked his own life in rescuing two drowning men.

Courtesy of North Carolina Collection

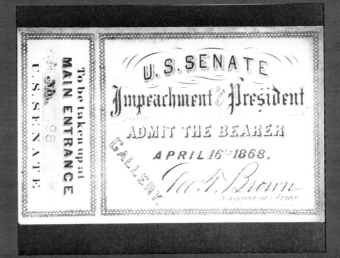

A ticket to the impeachment proceedings against
Andrew Johnson.
Courtesy of North Carolina State Archives

The determined seventeenth President, Raleigh-born
Andrew Johnson.
Courtesy of North Carolina State Archives

Leonidas Polk, son of Colonel William Polk and a native son of Raleigh. Chamberlain reports that as a boy he was known to have been a talented singer, and as a youth he was a keen student who entered the Military Academy at West Point in 1822. There, he was left cold and disheartened by the prevalent scorn for religious faith, and while at West Point, he himself grew more devout. He did graduate from the Military Academy, but went on to seminary school. In 1831 he was ordained deacon.

In time Leonidas Polk was consecrated Missionary Bishop of the Southwest, his diocese including Alabama, Mississippi, Louisiana, Arkansas, Texas, and the Territory of Oklahoma. Polk was a skillful and devoted evangelist who worked in the unsettled western part of our nation where there was generally little regard for religion. Frequently his life was threatened.

After the outbreak of civil war, Jefferson Davis asked Polk to serve the Confederacy. He became a general; the soldiers in his command loved him and called him "Bishop." He was killed in battle, outside of Atlanta, just before the close of the war.

Courtesy of North Carolina State Archives

Hubard's bronze replica of Houdon's marble statue of George Washington—dedicated in 1857 on Independence Day—was the first monument to be placed on the Capitol grounds.

Courtesy of North Carolina State Archives

This building is believed to have been the Raleigh Post Office, built in 1847, on Fayetteville Street. The compact temple-like styling was preferred by professional people of the day for offices, but the building soon became too small for the management of the city's mail. Dr. Fabius Haywood, Raleigh's first physician, bought the building for his own use, and he had it moved to South Street. The building is now maintained at the Mordecai Historic Park.

Courtesy of North Carolina State Archives

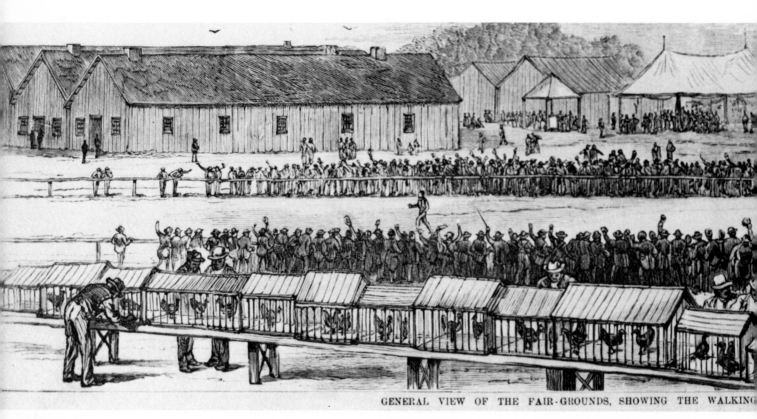

GENERAL VIEW OF THE FAIR-GROUNDS, SHOWING THE WALKING

At the time, the walking-match was a popular event throughout the nation. The drawing appeared in *Frank Leslie's Illustrated Newspaper,* 1879.

Courtesy of the North Carolina Collection

THE PROCESSION PASSING DOWN FAYETTEVILLE STREET, ON THE WAY TO THE GROUNDS.

In 1879, Raleigh was the scene of the first "colored industrial fair" held in the South. After this event other states followed the example set in North Carolina. This sketch of the fair procession passing down Fayetteville Street appeared in an 1879 edition of *Frank Leslie's Illustrated Newspaper.*

Courtesy of Raleigh News and Observer

BETWEEN NEGRO PEDESTRIANS.

WOOD CARTS, RALEIGH, NORTH CAROLINA.

Firewood could be bought by the bundle. This engraving showing farmers bringing their loaded oxcarts to town appeared in the September 16, 1871, edition of *Harper's Weekly.*

Courtesy of the North Carolina Collection

The sketch was made to depict the sport of cockfighting, though it would seem that friend and fowl alike have joined in the fray. This drawing appeared in an 1857 edition of *Harper's Magazine.* Such was one form of the general entertainment.

Courtesy of North Carolina State Archives

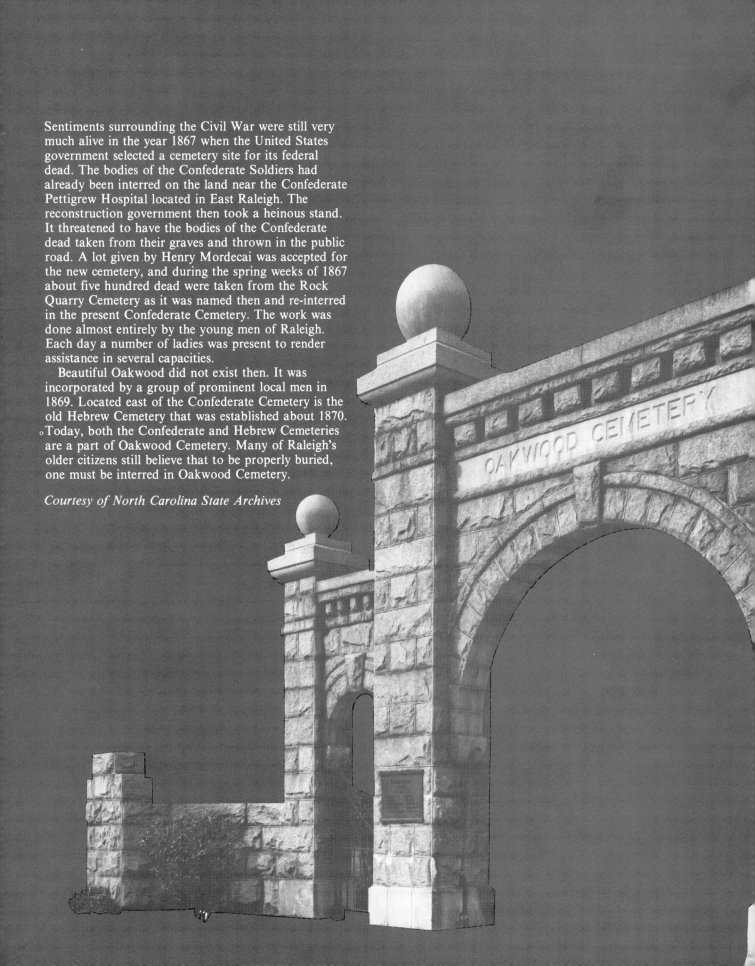

Sentiments surrounding the Civil War were still very much alive in the year 1867 when the United States government selected a cemetery site for its federal dead. The bodies of the Confederate Soldiers had already been interred on the land near the Confederate Pettigrew Hospital located in East Raleigh. The reconstruction government then took a heinous stand. It threatened to have the bodies of the Confederate dead taken from their graves and thrown in the public road. A lot given by Henry Mordecai was accepted for the new cemetery, and during the spring weeks of 1867 about five hundred dead were taken from the Rock Quarry Cemetery as it was named then and re-interred in the present Confederate Cemetery. The work was done almost entirely by the young men of Raleigh. Each day a number of ladies was present to render assistance in several capacities.

Beautiful Oakwood did not exist then. It was incorporated by a group of prominent local men in 1869. Located east of the Confederate Cemetery is the old Hebrew Cemetery that was established about 1870. Today, both the Confederate and Hebrew Cemeteries are a part of Oakwood Cemetery. Many of Raleigh's older citizens still believe that to be properly buried, one must be interred in Oakwood Cemetery.

Courtesy of North Carolina State Archives

Raleigh's first citizens placed their City Cemetery just beyond the eastern limits of the new town. The iron fence which had previously enclosed Capitol Square was eventually moved to the cemetery. Noted Raleigh citizens buried at the City Cemetery include Jacob Johnson, father of Andrew Johnson, John Rex, and Joseph Gales, one of the city's first newspaper editors.

Courtesy of North Carolina State Archives

In the Federal Cemetery, 1890.

Courtesy of North Carolina State Archives

Immense Central Prison was completed in 1883 by the labor of inmates. With its parapets, buttresses, and towers, the Penitentiary very much resembles a European castle. Stone for the prison's foundation was removed from the quarry shown in this early twentieth century photograph.

Courtesy of North Carolina State Archives

The prison cells, about 1910.

Courtesy of Duke University Manuscript Department

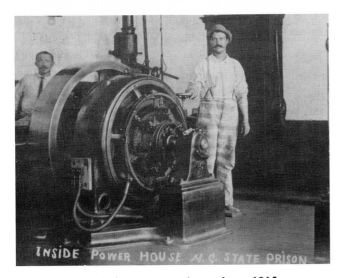

At the Central Prison power plant, about 1915.

Courtesy of the North Carolina Collection

Noticeable and often noticed for its flamboyant
architectural styling is the Heck-Andrews House of
Blount Street. It was built about 1870 for Colonel
Jonathan Heck, and it was kept by the Heck family
until 1921 when it became the property of A. B. Andrews,
who owned the house until 1946.

Courtesy of North Carolina State Archives

The Dodd-Hinsdale House of 330 Hillsborough Street was built in the late 1870s; its design has been admired for a century. The house was built in the Second Empire style with "Italianate" detailing, noticeable in the eaves. The future of the Dodd-Hinsdale House is uncertain; it may be taken down.

Courtesy of North Carolina State Archives

The Hawkins-Hartness House of 310 North Blount Street was built by Dr. William J. Hawkins as a surprise for his brother Dr. Alexander Boyd Hawkins and his wife Martha Hawkins.

Courtesy of North Carolina State Archives

Shown is Raleigh's first steamer. The city's first
firefighting company of the modern era was formed in
1870 as the Rescue Steam Fire Engine Company.
J. C. Brewster was the company foreman. Other
independent units were organized about this time,
including two black firefighting teams. By the end of
the 1870s, all the independent units were brought
together as the city's fire department.

Courtesy of Kenlon H. Brockwell

Shown are the officers of the Seventy-Second Regiment, led by the young Colonel John Wetmore Hinsdale, center photo. John W. Hinsdale bought the house at 330 Hillsborough Street in 1890 from William H. Dodd, who at one time was mayor of the city. Also shown are (2) Lieutenant Colonel W. Foster French; (3) First Lieutenant, Company K, W. W. King; (4) Second Lieutenant, Company C, J. W. Harper; (5) Second Lieutenant, Company C, H. W. Connelly; (6) Second Lieutenant, Company E, J. M. Bandy; (7) Second Lieutenant, Company K, D. S. Reid; (8) Orderly Sergeant, Company C, C. W. Taylor; (9) Private, Company B, J. L. McGimpsey.

Courtesy of Duke University Manuscript Department

The Seaboard Building has been used as a railroad office since 1862. The building, which displays some of Raleigh's finest ornamental ironwork, will be preserved as one of the city's landmarks.

Courtesy of the North Carolina Collection

In the drawing are Raleigh's Railroad Roundhouse and Foundry. Cars and coaches were repaired at the foundry, and reports indicate that coaches may have been manufactured there.

Courtesy of the North Carolina Collection

The Exposition Dining Hall.
Courtesy of North Carolina State Archives

The Wake County Exhibit included needlework, wood samples, portraits, photos of public buildings, a one hundred horsepower Watts Campbell Corliss Engine, and a fifty horsepower Harris Corliss Engine. One Wake County resident made a table using over sixty varieties of native wood.

Courtesy of North Carolina State Archives

The State Fair of 1884
The 1880s was an era of expositions, and after the notable
successes of expositions in Atlanta, Nashville, and
other cities, the State of North Carolina decided to
join in the competition for the coming prosperity. The
Fair of 1884 was a statewide exposition. Its purpose
was to show the "variety and magnificence" of North
Carolina's products, and to thereby attract "foreign"
industry, immigrants, and capital. "Foreign," by the
way, meant other states, such as Pennsylvania and
New York, as well as Europe.

Colonel W. S. Primrose and Stanhope Pullen were
among the Raleigh leaders to arouse the excitement and
energy for the exposition. The city formed a
Bureau of Intelligence to locate room and board for
out-of-towners. A new spur of the railroad line was
run to the exposition fairgrounds. Exhibits were set
up showing North Carolina products, minerals,
woods, cattle, fisheries, water power, transportation,
and vacation sports.

In all, the 1884 exposition was roundly praised. It
added to the pride of the city and the pride of the
state.

This group was photographed at the exposition. Just
what brought this crew together is currently
unfathomable.

Courtesy of North Carolina State Archives

Members of a local militia stand at attention at the
exposition. Such militia units were forerunners of our
present National Guard. One of their best-remembered
functions was the annual Military Ball.

Courtesy of the News and Observer

Bird's Eye View of A&M College. 1897 David Clark.

3rd Dormitory   2nd Dormitory   1st Dormitory   Watauga Hall   Barn Boiler House   Shops Dairy   Main Building

This 1897 drawing by David Clark shows the College of Agriculture and Mechanic Arts as it appeared in its early years. Bricks for the Main Building, the largest building in the drawing, were made at the State Prison. Later, the name of Main Building was changed to Holladay Hall. The dormitories were called first, second, third, and fourth, and they were designed to look like houses so that the students wouldn't feel they were far from home. At the dairy, the small building at the top right, the milk was placed in metal containers and was cooled by the running water of a creek.

Courtesy of North Carolina State University Archives

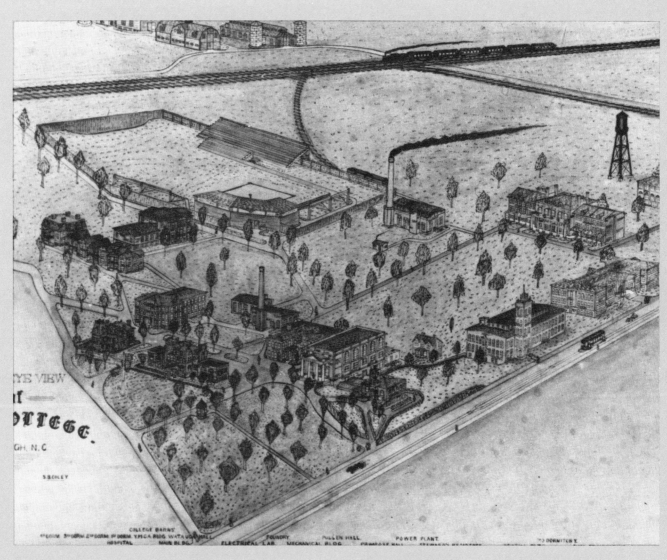

Another "Bird's Eye View" of A and M College, this one drawn by S. B. Coley in 1911, and when compared with the previous drawing, it shows the school's rapid growth.

Courtesy of North Carolina State University Archives

Holladay Hall, still standing and still in use on the North Carolina State University campus, was named for the school's first president, Alexander Q. Holladay. It was erected in 1889, and was the school's first building. This photo shows the building about 1910.

Courtesy of North Carolina State Archives

This photograph shows the graduating members of the Class of 1893 of the North Carolina College of Agriculture and Mechanic Arts. These students were the school's first graduates. A and M, of course, grew to become North Carolina State University.

In the top row, from left to right are S. C. Asbury, W. M. N. Lytch, W. H. Turner, F. T. Meacham, J. W. McKay, C. D. Franks, C. B. Holliday, W. J. Matthews, C. E. Seymore, and G. P. Gray. In the middle row are S. M. Young, R. W. Allen, College President Alexander Q. Holladay, C. B. Williams, and B. W. Thorne. E. M. Gibbon, H. E. Bonitz, C. D. Sellers, L. T. Yarborough, and F. F. Floyd are in the bottom row.

Courtesy of North Carolina State University Archives

The A and M baseball team of 1899. In the top row from left to right are players W. M. Person, Bill Fenner, Manager Ned Wood, J. W. Shore, Norman, and Lewis. In the bottom row are Dorsett, F. D. Ross, Faison, Casserby, and F. W. Bonitz.

The little fellow in the middle of the group picture was Wallace Riddick, who appears to have been befriended by the team. His father, Wallace Carl Riddick, was college president from 1916 until 1923.

Courtesy of North Carolina State University Archives

Estey Hall is the oldest surviving building on the Shaw University campus, having been erected in 1873 to house women students. The education of blacks was begun at Shaw in the post-Civil War years. The photo dates to about 1890.

Courtesy of North Carolina State Archives

Raleigh's Shaw University supported the nation's first black medical school. Leonard Medical School was opened in 1882. The photos show the Victorian and imposing Medical Building and the Medical Dormitory, where the students are playing croquet. Both photos date to the 1890s.

Courtesy of North Carolina State Archives

In 1857, the eighty-four year old bachelor William Peace was among those who provided funds for the establishment of a school for girls. Though the building was finished before the Civil War, it would be many years before classes were held. During the Civil War the building served as a military hospital, and after the war it held the Freedman's Bureau. It was not until 1872 that the school was opened. In 1879 Peace Institute had the first kindergarten in the south. The school is now known as Peace College. This 1872 drawing was used in the school's first catalogues.

Courtesy of Peace College

This photo of the Raleigh Male Academy and its students was taken in 1891. The school's principal at the time was Professor Hugh Morson, who in later years would serve as principal of Raleigh's first High School.

Courtesy of North Carolina State Archives

Saint Augustine's campus as it appeared about 1900. Saint Augustine's Normal and Collegiate Institute was formed in 1867 through the work of the Episcopal Diocese of North Carolina, the Freedman's Commission of the Protestant Episcopal Church, and the Freedman's Bureau. The school's original purpose was to educate blacks rising from slavery. The first principal was Reverend Jacob Brinton Smith, and when first opened, the school had four students.

On the far left in the photograph is Taylor Hall, which served as the school's first library. The next building is the Chapel, and to its right is the Lyman Building, which served as a boys' dormitory.

Courtesy of Saint Augustine's College

A closer look at Taylor Hall on the Saint Augustine's campus. This building, the Lyman building, and the Chapel were almost entirely constructed by student classes in the building trades. Undoubtedly, the people in this picture, taken at about the turn of the century, were among those who helped build Taylor Hall.

Courtesy of Saint Augustine's College

Raleigh's "Championship" Volunteer Rescue Steam Fire Engine Company of 1890 was photographed by Will Wynne at the fire station which stood on Fayetteville Street about where the Insurance Building is now located. The "Championship" was won in a statewide competition in which the various companies raced to attach a section of hose to a terminal and then to pump up enough pressure to start the water flowing.

Courtesy of North Carolina State Archives

The Caraleigh Cotton Mill began operation in 1892. The mill brought about the development of the Caraleigh community. Average salaries for the mill workers in its first years amounted to about twelve or thirteen dollars a week, and children of ten to twelve years of age received ten cents a day.

In the late 1920s the mill was forced to close with the coming of economic depression, and so there was little work for a community of mill workers. This time of privation drew the Caraleigh residents together and intensified their community loyalties. The mill re-opened in 1938, has changed ownership several times, and is now run by the Fred Whitaker Company.

Courtesy of North Carolina State Archives

The old State Fish Hatcheries.

Courtesy of North Carolina State Archives

The Water Tower as photographed in the early 1960s.

Courtesy of North Carolina State Archives

This is believed to be the oldest existing photograph of the Morgan Street Water Tower, dating to about 1890. Reinforced concrete and steel were not used at the time of the tower's construction in 1887, and so its walls of granite and brick were made more than three feet thick. Years ago, the water tank would occasionally overflow. This delighted the schoolchildren next door at the High School.

Courtesy of North Carolina State Archives

Raleigh did not have a successful city water supply and water works until the 1880s. Several fires within the city made the need for such a system quite apparent. Then, too, other communities had built systems and there were those in Raleigh who did not wish to see their city lag behind. In this era of industrial advance, progress and pride often served to spur one another. These photos, taken in the early 1890s, show the pumping station and the filtration plant.

Courtesy of North Carolina State Archives

The Governor's Mansion

A simple frame house was to serve as the first official residence of North Carolina Governors. But in 1816, the governor's residence was established at a large brick "palace" situated at the foot of Fayetteville Street. In 1825, General Lafayette, on a visit to Raleigh, stayed at the "palace." Sherman was to use this residence as his headquarters after the Civil War, and when he withdrew, he left it "in a state of destruction." It was never again to be the home of a North Carolina governor; from 1871 through 1891 the state's chief executives would either rent homes or stay at the city's most famous hotel, the Yarborough House.

The problem of providing a suitable residence for the Governor came before a state legislative committee as early as 1877, but it was not until 1883, upon the urgings of Governor Jarvis, that construction of a mansion, to be built upon Burke Square, was finally authorized. In his original plan for the city, William Christmas had suggested that Burke Square could serve as an appropriate location for a governor's home.

The original plans for the mansion, as drawn by Sloan, were only to be slightly modified. Construction was done largely by convicts from the state penitentiary. Many of these convicts inscribed their names or initials in the bricks used in the building itself and in its walks. In 1891, Governor Daniel G. Fowle became the mansion's first occupant.

The mansion, architecturally, is a combination of Queen Anne and Eastlake styles. As described in the North Carolina Museum: "Vital to both architectural forms, and this is especially evident at the Executive Mansion, is the lively way in which the irregular massing, elaborate ornament, and rich color respond to the play of light and shadow. Each element works with the changing light to create a variety of patterns so that the character of the building changes at different times of day and year." Franklin Delano Roosevelt was to call North Carolina's Executive Mansion "the most beautiful in America."

Known throughout the state as the "Governor's Palace," this mansion would serve as the home of North Carolina Governors from 1816 until the Civil War. It stood at the foot of Fayetteville Street, at the opposite end of the street from the Capitol. Immediately after the Civil War, Sherman set up headquarters in the "Palace," and when his occupation was ended, he left the mansion in such a disrupted condition that it was never again to house a North Carolina governor.

Courtesy of North Carolina State Archives

The Yarborough House was a favorite place of lodging for politicians who came to the city in the latter half of the nineteenth century and the first quarter of this century. From 1871 until 1889 it would often serve as the unofficial residence of North Carolina's Governors.

Courtesy of the State Division of Travel and Promotion

A 1908 postcard bearing a picture of the Governor's Mansion. In recent years, an enclosing wall has been placed about the Mansion's grounds for reasons of security.

The Executive Mansion Dining Hall as photographed
by Albert Barden in 1941.

Courtesy of North Carolina State Archives

A convict named Williams clearly inscribed his name
in one of the bricks which forms the walks
surrounding the Mansion.

Courtesy of North Carolina State Archives

At the unveiling of the Confederate Monument on the
Capitol grounds, May 20, 1895.

Courtesy of Duke University Manuscript Department

EIGH, N. C,   Confederate Monument   3187

This photo, taken about 1910, shows the Confederate
Monument before the west entrance to the Capitol. Its
cornerstone was laid in 1894. The monument is
formed of a seventy-five foot shaft of Mount Airy
granite topped and flanked by bronze statues of
Confederate soldiers, which were done by the
Bavarian sculptor Ferdinand Van Miller.

Courtesy of the North Carolina Collection

The citizens of Raleigh, on this day in 1893, have gathered on Fayetteville Street to pay final respects to Confederate President Jefferson Davis. Having come from Louisiana on its way to re-interment in Richmond, the body was rested for several days in the Capitol.

Courtesy of North Carolina State Archives

Christ Church was photographed in 1909. The church's first rector was Bishop John Stark Ravenscroft, who, when a young man, has been described in the church's literature as "utterly careless and reckless of all religious restraints, a man of the world, soulless and profane. He had been called Mad Jack by his college mates at William and Mary." Due to his early experiences, he was later able to write to another member of the clergy, Brother Green, that "I have one advantage over you; while you were brought up in the fear of God and in ignorance of the great wickedness that is going on in the world, I know all about the ways of sinners and can therefore track the scoundrels into all their dens and hiding places and strip them of their self-conceit and refuge of lies."

As a rector, Ravenscroft attached great importance to proper decorum. While traveling in a coach, Ravenscroft was once in the company of a man whose language was rife with profanity. He asked this man, several times, to amend his speech, but the man's language only grew more and more offensive. The very tall and two hundred and twenty pound Ravenscroft then pronounced: "Utter another oath, sir, if you dare, and I will throw you under the wheels of this coach," and found that his companion grew quiet.

What has been related, though perhaps adding color, is not intended to paint a complete picture of the devoted and capable first rector of Christ Church.

Courtesy of North Carolina State Archives

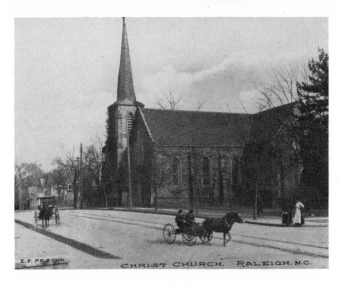

Christ Church, as photographed for one of the city's postcards in the 1890s. Raleigh's splendid Christ Church is a notable example of Gothic Revival architectural form that was often used at the time of its construction in the 1850s. Atop the church steeple is a weathercock, which cannot be seen in this photograph. When Sherman's troops finally left Raleigh, this was said to be the only chicken in town.

Courtesy of Duke University Manuscript Department

The First Presbyterian Church has been located at Salisbury Street across from Capitol Square since 1818. The present day structure was dedicated in 1900.

Courtesy of North Carolina State Archives

Saint Augustine's Church was built at Lane and Dawson Streets as the house of worship for the students of Saint Augustine's College. The school built a chapel on its campus shortly before the start of the twentieth century, and this building was moved to South Wilmington Street in 1901. At about this point, the Church became known as Saint Ambrose. There were those who felt that the most elaborate services in the city were held here. The little church was taken down in 1965.

Courtesy of Olivia Raney Library

The Olivia Raney Library was given to the city of Raleigh by Richard Beverly Raney in memory of his beloved wife. Because of its origin, the splendid building which stood at the corner of Hillsborough and Salisbury Streets was considered to be Raleigh's Taj Mahal.

Early in life, Raney was a clerk at the Yarborough House. Eventually, he would become president of the Raleigh Chamber of Commerce, a Vice President of the Standard Gas and Electric Company, and he would serve as the General Agent for North Carolina of the Penn Mutual Life Insurance Company.

Upon the death of his wife, the former Olivia Cowper, to whom he had been married for only a year and a half, Raney offered to make a gift of the library. He was responsible for having the library built, equipped, decorated, and furnished. The postcard here appears to have been mailed in 1907.

Courtesy of North Carolina State Archives

One would come to this, the second floor of the Olivia Raney Library, to choose and read books. The librarian's quarters were on the first floor, and an auditorium with a stage was on the third floor, where dances were held. This photograph, made about the turn of the century, was likely taken before the library was opened to the public in 1901.

Courtesy of the Olivia Raney Library

Olivia Cowper Raney, 1861-1896, as painted by Mrs. Lesley Bush-Brown. In her lifetime, Olivia Raney devoted herself to many charitable undertakings. Upon her death, those who worked with her wrote: "The poor, the sick, the oppressed have lost a friend who never failed to hear their suffering cry. Her soft graciousness, her great heart, her devotion to duty, her noble example of Christian living shall always be a precious and endearing memory."

Courtesy of the Olivia Raney Library

Photo by Jackson Hill

Saint Agnes Hospital was dedicated on October 18,
St. Luke's Day, in 1896. Mrs. Aaron Burtis Hunter,
wife of the principal of Saint Augustine's, made an
appeal for the needed hospital facility at the General
Convention of the Protestant Episcopal Church in
1895, and her appeal was answered with two
donations, of five and six hundred dollars. The
hospital's first patient had malarial fever and was
cured. The first baby born in the hospital, the
daughter of Mr. and Mrs. A. J. Griffin, was named
Agnes, and she eventually became a physician.

Courtesy of Saint Augustine's College

When the Saint Agnes Hospital facility became too
small to properly accommodate its patients, Mrs.
Hunter again campaigned to raise funds for a larger,
more modern facility. This time over forty thousand
dollars was collected. Stone for the building was
quarried on the Saint Augustine's campus, and the
new St. Agnes Hospital, pictured here, was opened in
1909. In later years, three-fourths of its patients were
charity cases. The hospital finally ceased operation in
1959, and the building is still used to hold offices of Saint
Augustine's College.

Courtesy of North Carolina State Archives

The Class of 1896 at Peace Institute. The young ladies in the front row, from left to right, are Beulah Witherspoon, Edith Butler, Knox Johnson, and Minnie Mangum. In the back row are Nattie Simms, Mary Yancey, Mary Rankin, Mabel Ramsey, Kate Lewis, and Cora Richardson.

The first girl to enroll at Peace was Katharine Bryan Sloan, who would become the mother of Frank Porter Graham, the first President of the Consolidated University of North Carolina.

Courtesy of Peace College

The State School for the Blind, shown here as it appeared about 1900, was situated at the corner of Jones and Dawson Streets. The building was later used to house the State Board of Health, and today part of the original building is still used by the state to house the Department of Natural and Economic Resources.

Courtesy of the Duke University Manuscript Department

Troubles with transportation, at the home of Will
Robbin on Hillsborough Street, at the turn of the
century.

Courtesy of North Carolina Museum of Natural History

These students and teachers were photographed before
the West Rock building on the Saint Mary's Campus,
and the occasion appears to have been graduation in
May of 1900. Among those in the photo are Freda
Hills, Mary Philips, Helen Gray, Belle Nash, Pearl
Pratt, Julia Parsley, Sue Hayes, Addie Gaylord, Alma
Smith, Addie Moore, Sally Leach, Sue Hayes, Kate
Hedgepeth, and Mary Bunn.

Courtesy of Saint Mary's College

This early twentieth century postcard provides views of Pullen Park, which was the generous gift to the city of Stanhope Pullen. Pullen Park, of course, now adjoins the campus of North Carolina State University. Stanhope Pullen was certainly one individual who practiced the Christian ideals of charity in his everyday life, and the same may be said of his nephew, John T. Pullen. On a cold day, John T. Pullen was seen taking off his coat and giving it to a poor man who did not have a proper winter garment.

Courtesy of Duke University Manuscript Department

The Pullen Park Lily Pond, 1904.

Courtesy of North Carolina State Archives

About 1903, Albert Barden took this remarkable
photograph of a Negro baptism service in Wake
County. Such services were held annually, and those
who felt that they had become sullied in the course of
twelve months were able to participate in the cleansing
ritual each year.

Courtesy of North Carolina State Archives

The 200 block of Fayetteville Street is shown after the Great Snow of 1899, which lasted for three days. Notice the horse and sleigh in the street. This was probably one of the few sleighs in the city. The bearded fellow was John C. Stedman Lumsden.

Courtesy of North Carolina State Archives

Looking from the Capitol grounds to Edenton Street,
shortly before the turn of the century. The building on
the left is the Labor Building, on the right is the
Agriculture Building. As can be guessed by looking at
the Labor Building, it was a two-story structure.
Without making the building taller, two floors were
later added inside, and the Labor Building became a
four-story structure. The Agriculture Building had
served as the Eagle Hotel, the National Hotel, and as
Guion's Hotel before it was bought by the state in the
late 1880s.

Courtesy of the North Carolina Collection

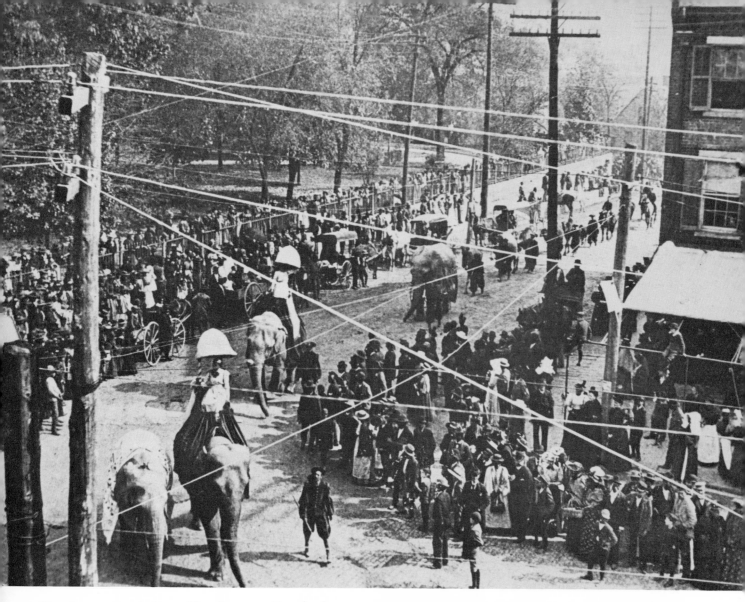

The circus comes to town. The circus would arrive by train and assemble itself on Johnson Street while a delighted crowd watched. One young fellow once gave an elephant a plug of tobacco, causing the animal to choke. But this elephant didn't forget his tormentor. He stalked off to the nearest mud puddle, filled his trunk, turned back, and just about washed that boy away.

Courtesy of the Raleigh News and Observer

It wouldn't seem that this photo of young boys with their goat-cart was taken at any other time than on a summer afternoon.

Courtesy of the Raleigh News and Observer

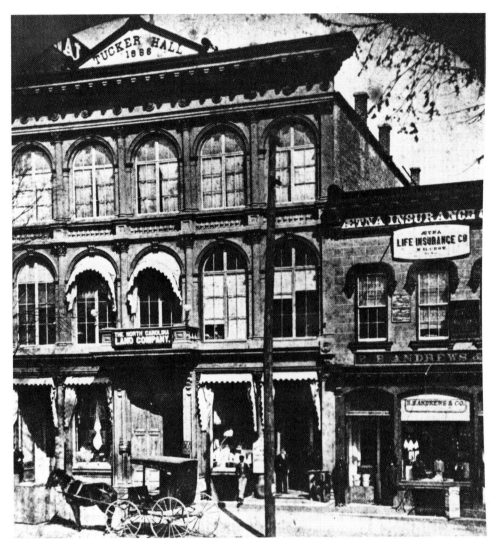

Tucker Hall, in the vicinity of Morgan and Hargett Streets, housed many of the city's entertainments. In the times before the movies, vaudeville troups, traveling repertory companies, and musicians would perform on the top floor at Tucker Hall. When plays were presented, a singer would come on stage between acts. "The Last Rose of Summer," or another such song with trills, would be a likely choice for sopranos and would-be sopranos.

On the first floor of Tucker Hall, in this photo from the early 1900s, you can see the North Carolina Land Company. Such companies would promote the development of new communities in the state, and in conjunction with the railroad companies they would plan excursions to the sites of the planned communities. Train excursions were quite the rage in the 1890s. A Norfolk excursion group once came to Raleigh, toured the city, had its own parade, and then rode back to Norfolk.

Courtesy of North Carolina State Archives

The trolley was photographed at the head of Fayetteville Street. Raleigh had four miles of horse-drawn trolley tracks by the late 1880s. The city aldermen, in 1890, voted to add two miles of track and convert to an electric system. A contract was signed with Edison Electric, and the first electric car ran on Hillsborough Street in September of 1891.

Courtesy of North Carolina State Archives

BASEBALL
TO-DAY
FAYETTEVILLE
to
RALEIGH

Looking west from the residential 300 block of Hillsborough Street.

Courtesy of North Carolina State Archives

Raleigh's old combination City Hall and Market House stood between Exchange Street and Market Place. Market goods were sold on the first floor, court and the mayor's quarters were on the second floor, and the police department and the jail occupied the basement. Movies were also shown upstairs, and in the years after this photo was made, there are those who remember seeing Charlie Chaplin, Fatty Arbuckle, and Mack Sennet. The large horn of a Victor Talking Machine protruded through a window, and music was played to lure those passing by to come in and watch a movie.

This photo, from the first of this century, was likely taken on a Sunday, for on all other days, wagons loaded with produce would have been lined at the side of the building.

Courtesy of North Carolina State Archives

This city's Post Office was the first to be built in the South after the Civil War. As it now approaches its one hundredth year, it has become known as the Century Post Office. Completed in 1878, it has been remodeled over the years.

Courtesy of North Carolina State Archives

The town house of Dr. Fabius Haywood stood at the southwest corner of Morgan and Fayetteville Streets. It was built in 1818, and was taken down in 1911 to make room for state government offices. Ironically, offices of the State Department of History were among those that took the place of this structure from Raleigh's past.

Courtesy of North Carolina State Archives

The Raleigh National Bank Building was built at the corner of West Hargett and Fayetteville Streets about 1868 and was known familiarly as the "Round Steps Bank." At the time of this photograph, the facility belonged to the Raleigh Banking and Trust Company. A 1910 Chamber of Commerce publication estimated that the bank's resources at the time amounted to about three quarters of a million dollars.

Courtesy of North Carolina State Archives

Ensign Worth Bagley, the brother of Mrs. Josephus Daniels, was the first American naval officer to fall in the Spanish-American War. Bagley was buried at Oakwood Cemetery. This monument was erected in 1908 on Capitol Square.

Courtesy of the North Carolina Collection

The Dr. Andrew Goodwin house was built at 220 Hillsborough Street in 1903. Goodwin was Head Physician at Saint Agnes Hospital, and he was also associated with Leonard Medical School. The house was used for several years by Kings Business College.

The Baptist Female University stood at the corner of
Blount and Edenton Streets. This, the Main Building,
was the entire school, containing lodgings, classrooms,
laboratories, chapel, dining room, and library. In 1909
the school changed its name to Meredith College, and
the college was moved to its present location in 1926.

Courtesy of the North Carolina Collection

Thomas Meredith was the first to sponsor the idea for a Baptist College for Women, making his proposal in 1838 at the Baptist State Convention.

Courtesy of the North Carolina Collection

Johnson Hall, the administration building of the present Meredith College which is situated upon 220 acres at 3800 Hillsborough Street. Meredith College is now the largest church-related women's college in the south.

Courtesy of Meredith College

Rex Hospital

John Rex was a tanner who lived in Raleigh through the first decades of the nineteenth century. He felt that a community was obliged to provide care for its sick, and wrote of the need for a hospital in editorials in the city newspapers. When Rex died, he left a sum of money, to be managed by trustees, for the establishment of a hospital. In 1861, trustees of the Rex estate invested in Confederate War Bonds, and so at the close of the war, the trust was nearly bankrupt. In later years, trustees were eventually able to make financial gains, and fifty-five years after the death of John Rex, the first Rex hospital was opened.

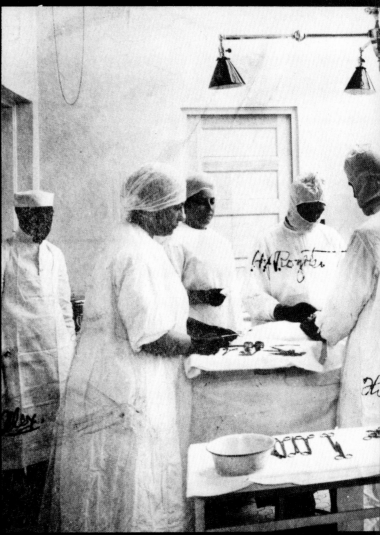

The Governor Manly House on South Street, close to Salisbury Street, served as the first Rex Hospital. The building was bought from the St. John's Guild of the Church of the Good Shepherd in 1893 for 4,500 dollars. Rex Hospital opened in 1894.

Courtesy of North Carolina State Archives

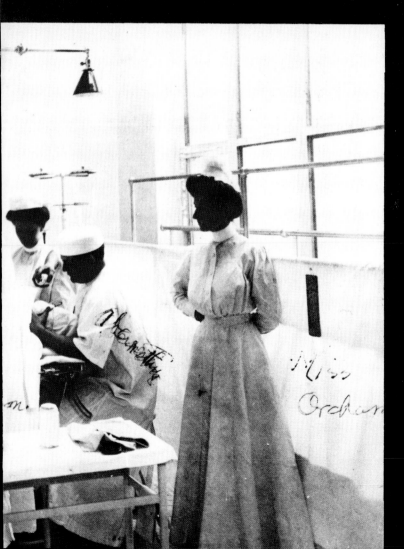

In the Rex Hospital operating room, 1909. Dr. Hubert Royster, fourth from the left, was the Hospital's Chief Surgeon, as he was the only surgeon, and Dr. Abernethy, 'second from the right, had charge of anesthesia.

Courtesy of North Carolina State Archives

The Manly House was taken down in 1908 to make room for a larger hospital facility. The second of Raleigh's Rex Hospitals opened in 1909, and was originally built to hold sixty beds.

Courtesy of North Carolina State Archives

A 1937 photograph of the present Rex Hospital, taken about the time this third facility was completed.

Courtesy of Rex Hospital

Rex Hospital on Wade Avenue and Saint Mary's
Street, as photographed in 1972, showing the addition
of extensions and outbuildings. South wing has been
added since the time of this photo.

Courtesy of Rex Hospital

Fayetteville Street awaits the State Fair Parade in
1909, and in the 1921 photo, the parade marches up
the street to turn down Morgan. In the 1921 photo,
the Fair Marshalls ride the horses.

Courtesy of the North Carolina Collection

Courtesy of
North Carolina State Archives

The Water Tower is in the background, William Gaston's law office can be seen in front of the tower, and in the foreground is the hearse that carried the body of John Brown, in this photograph taken about 1910.

Courtesy of North Carolina State Archives

The Rudy and Buffaloe Cash Grocery Store on 108 East Hargett Street carried a "splendid line of fancy and staple groceries, canned goods and table delicacies, as well as salt meats of all kinds and also a good line of imported and domestic cigars and tobacco." The firm's policy was to use cash in buying and selling every product, and this was done to provide "low prices and reliable goods" for the city's housekeepers.

Courtesy of Raleigh Chamber of Commerce

The Masonic Temple Building, one of Raleigh's first "skyscrapers," still holds offices.

Courtesy of Duke University Manuscript Department

The Norwood Cigar Company was established by J. M. Norwood at 105 West Martin Street in 1887. After 1900, they were known to maintain a large supply of Dixie Smokers, "a five cent cigar of exceptional merit."

Courtesy of Raleigh Chamber of Commerce

Shown are front and side views of the Academy of Music Building, the scene of many of the city's entertainments. It was built in 1893 at 302-304 South Salisbury Street, and the first presentation included a dramatic portrayal of Sir Walter Raleigh's landing at Roanoke Island. According to the WPA booklet, this aroused considerable comment, for Raleigh never came to mainland North Carolina. In 1910, there was nearly a riot, and the police were summoned after Raleigh leaders had refused to allow the presentation of *The Girl from Rector's,* a production deemed to exceed the limits of propriety.

Courtesy of Raleigh News and Observer

The Mikado, presented by a local theatre group at the
Academy of Music.

Courtesy of Kenlon H. Brockwell

A local minstrel group is shown on stage at the
Academy of Music Building. On the far right in black
face is Sherwood Brockwell. Brockwell was once
offered a contract to play big league baseball, but he
refused the contract, not wanting to leave Raleigh.

Courtesy of Kenlon H. Brockwell

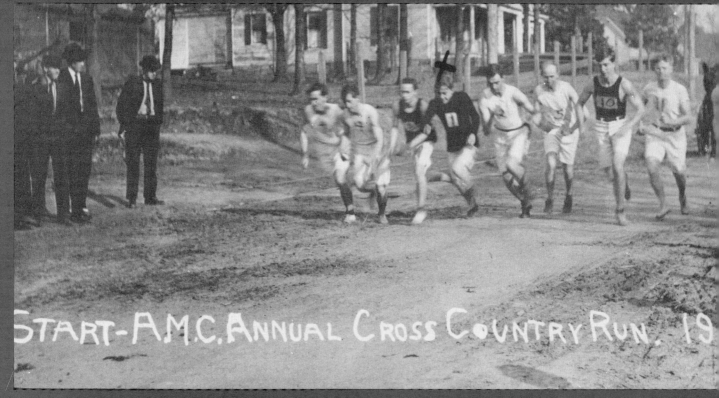

START-A.M.C. ANNUAL CROSS COUNTRY RUN. 19

Start and finish of the annual cross country meet held
by the Agriculture and Mechanic College, 1910. The
eventual winner is marked in the first photograph.

Courtesy of North Carolina State University Archives

The A and M College Dramatics Club, in 1903,
presented *She Stoops to Conquer*. The tall fellow with
the long-haired wig standing in the center was O. Max
Gardner, who became governor of the state.

Courtesy of North Carolina State University Archives

FINISH A.M.C. ANNUAL CROSS COUNTRY RUN 1910

About 1910, students at A and M ate their meals in Pullen Hall. But this building was not originally made to hold a cafeteria, and consequently it had no cooking facilities. The food was prepared in a temporary lean-to structure, and was transported to the Pullen Hall dining room. Pullen Hall was destroyed by fire in 1965.

Courtesy of North Carolina State University Archives

From left to right are Mary Sherwood, Fleming Sherwood, and Grace Bates. The woman in back was not identified. The photo was taken at 214 East Morgan Street, circa 1910.

Courtesy of Frank Sherwood

Francis W. Sherwood is at work in this 1910 photograph at the North Carolina Agriculture Experiment Station chemistry laboratory at A and M College.

Courtesy of Frank Sherwood

At the same address, this lovely photo was taken of Mary Bates Sherwood. The property now belongs to the state government.

Courtesy of Frank Sherwood

HOTEL RALEIGH.

The Hotel Raleigh's proximity to the Union Depot made it a convenient stopping place for travelers and tourists. By 1910 it contained 110 rooms, sixty-five private baths, and a dining room that could seat one hundred guests. Because it faced Nash Square, it was originally called the Park Hotel. In 1919, the hotel could boast of providing "every comfort and convenience, including up-to-date elevator service."

Courtesy of the North Carolina Collection

The decorative parlor of the Hotel Raleigh.

Courtesy of the North Carolina Collection

Aunt Betsy Holmes and her Horseless Carriage, Raleigh, N. C.

During the first decade of the twentieth century, Aunt Betsy Holmes and her horseless carriage were a pleasantly familiar sight. She was so widely known that postcards were made bearing her photograph. The writing on one such postcard, made about 1910, stated that "Although almost a centurion, Aunt Betsy is an active daily worker on a little farm of a few acres four miles north of Raleigh. She has never known sickness and the sunshine of her expansive smile has made her famous."

Courtesy of Duke University Manuscript Department

This picture of the Coca-Cola Bottling Works on 115 South Wilmington Street might provide a suitable place to tell a story about Tim Lee. Tim was sheriff during the Civil War, and on one occasion he had to serve a writ upon an individual who lived sixty-four miles from Raleigh. The question arose as to how long it would take him to cover the distance. Tim is said to have bet a considerable sum, five thousand dollars, that he would leave Raleigh, serve the writ, and return, all between sunup and sundown.

He left Raleigh at sunrise in a sulky and driving tandem. He took five bottles of whisky. After covering half the distance, he gave the horses a bottle of whisky each in their mash; when he reached his destination he gave the horses half a bottle each, and half way back home, each horse was given another bottle. One horse collapsed, the other survived, and Tim Lee won his bet.

Courtesy of Raleigh Chamber of Commerce

Woodall's Stables were opened on the corner of Davie and Blount Streets in 1910. Owners L. H. Woodall and J. V. Marr accorded prospective customers the right to personally inspect the premises. As written in the Chamber of Commerce publication of 1910, the "firm invites everyone whose horse needs a holiday to send him to them. He will look better, feel better and drive better after being under their care for a short time."

Courtesy of Raleigh Chamber of Commerce

The Carolina Garage and Machine Company was formed in 1909 on West Hargett Street to succeed and consolidate the businesses of W. C. Brewer and John A. Park. The company operated the largest garage in the state, employing eleven mechanics. Here, you could purchase a Buick, Franklin, Waverly, or White. John A. Park, the firm's secretary and manager, taught mathematics for four years at A and M before entering the automobile business. Shop superintendent W. C. Gill was described as a "practical man and an expert on automobiles."

Courtesy of Raleigh Chamber of Commerce

Shorty Brown, one of Raleigh's first chauffeurs, sits behind the wheel of a 1913 Ford roadster.

Courtesy of Raleigh News and Observer

The cornerstone of this, the oldest standing brick building in the city, was laid March 23, 1813. In 1814, when the building was completed, it was occupied by the State Bank of North Carolina. In 1873 it was sold to Christ Church for use as the rectory of Dr. Richard S. Mason. It has been known both as the State Bank Building and as the State Bank Rectory.

In this 1911 photograph, the boys sitting on the steps most likely attended Sunday School classes at the State Bank Rectory.

Courtesy of the North Carolina Collection

Raleigh's combination City Hall and City Auditorium on Davie Street was built in 1910 at a cost of 125 thousand dollars. In the photograph, the figures of the pedestrians were drawn in.

Courtesy of Duke University Manuscript Department

The State Bank Building of New Bern Avenue. Now owned by the North Carolina National Bank, it houses the State Bicentennial Headquarters.

Courtesy of North Carolina State Archives

The Northeast corner of Martin and Fayetteville Streets has been occupied by a bank since the time of the Civil War. The Citizens National Bank built a four story building there in 1871, and the building in this photograph was erected by the same bank in 1912. Citizens National sold to the North Carolina National Bank and Trust Company. When this banking company went under in the depression year 1933, the Security National Bank moved into the building. In 1960 Security National Bank merged with the North Carolina National Bank, the old bank building was finally taken down, and the present NCNB building was finished in 1966.

In this 1914 photograph, the Wake County Savings Bank is in the white building next to the Citizens National Bank, and next to Wake County Savings is Galloway's Drug Store. The wagon in the foreground belonged to Mr. Fleming, who sold bags of peanuts and buttered popcorn for five cents.

Courtesy of North Carolina State Archives

Looking north toward the Capitol from the 200 block of Fayetteville Street, 1912. The Western Union messengers kept their bicycles parked on the sidewalk. Briggs Hardware Building, the fourth on the left, has been serving Raleigh since 1874.

Courtesy of North Carolina State Archives

Peering through the telephone wire and looking north toward the 200 block of Fayetteville Street, 1912. Horse and carriage pass unhurriedly before an approaching trolley car. In 1879 an Edison telephone system was set up, and Raleigh became the first city in North Carolina to have this facility. The Edison system was replaced by a Bell Telephone system in 1881. By 1890, the city had more than 170 telephone customers.

Courtesy of North Carolina State Archives

At the switchboard of the Raleigh Telephone Company Inc., 1910. From 1899 to 1915 Raleigh was the only city or town in the nation that had three separate telephone exchanges. Competition among the three companies was fierce, and in order to keep all channels of communication open, leading businessmen were forced to install three phones. This confusing condition was somewhat alleviated when the Interstate Company sold to Bell in 1915, and the matter was entirely remedied when the Raleigh Telephone Company did the same in 1922.

Courtesy of Raleigh Chamber of Commerce

The depression in the road on the one hundred block of West Martin Street, as you look east, was known as "foggy bottom." There is some disagreement as to just why this name was applied to the spot. Some say it was because the fog collected at this low point while others recall that the neighborhood was notorious for its saloons, and the city's tramps could usually be found here. The photo was taken about 1914.

Courtesy of North Carolina State Archives

This 1911 photograph shows the Boylan-Pearce store as it stood on the 200 block of Fayetteville Street. Notice the detailed quoined corners on the left side of this building. This styling is a reminder of days when homes were made of wooden logs, and the ends of the logs extended past the building's corner.

In the 1890s, a Boylan-Pearce advertisement stated that the store carried everything one could possibly need for the beach, including telescopes. Telescopes were collapsible suitcases.

Courtesy of North Carolina State Archives

A little trading and talking among the cotton buyers in front of the Commercial Bank Building, about 1913. From left to right are L. M. Parker, Senior, George Whitaker, George Taylor, W. R. Newsome, Joe H. Weathers, C. L. Hinton, Claude D. Barbee, M. L. Whitaker and T. A. Whitaker.

Raleigh leaders of the 1880s and 1890s had dreams of the city growing to take a place among the largest metropolises in the South. Building a cotton mill seemed a necessary step in the realization of this dream. Shares were sold, and the first cotton mill was built in Raleigh by about 1890. Of course, Raleigh never did become a huge metropolis like Atlanta, but the 1890s were years of rapid growth. Leaders of commerce in the city regretted that the manufacture of bright leaf tobacco never took hold in Raleigh as it had in the newer industrial town of Durham.

Courtesy of North Carolina State Archives

August 24, 1914, the force of the *Raleigh Times* news carriers lines up.

Courtesy of North Carolina State Archives

Raleigh had a volunteer fire department until 1913, and this photo shows some of the city's first paid firefighters. In the photo are George Aikens, Walter Moore, Lassiter, Charles Farmer, C. F. Gaston, Luther Thomason, Earnest Holland, Eugene Jones, Henry Parrish, and Mathews Barker. Sherwood Brockwell, passenger in the center vehicle, was the first full-time paid fire chief in America.

Courtesy of North Carolina State Archives

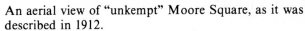

An aerial view of "unkempt" Moore Square, as it was described in 1912.

Courtesy of North Carolina State Archives

Halifax Street stretches away in this photograph taken from the roof of the Capitol about 1890. The sky is covered by cloud, the ground by snow. You can see the iron fence that used to surround the Capitol.

On snowy days in those times before World War I, the boys at A and M would build bobsleds and hitch them behind the street cars to get a free ride down Hillsborough Street. The conductor would usually be reluctant to put a stop to this practice, for, as one fellow has mentioned, "There were more of us than there was of him."

Courtesy of North Carolina State Archives

One of the hand-carved wooden figures of the Pullen
Park merry-go-round which has delighted young
Raleigh citizens since 1912. It is now a historic site.

Photo by Jackson Hill

Bloomsbury Park

Bloomsbury Park opened in 1912, and there are still Raleigh citizens who have fond memories of their childhood associated with it. Bloomsbury covered one hundred acres in the vicinity of the Carolina Country Club and Country Club Hills, and the pond, where once you could take a boat ride, now serves as a golf course water hazard. The park was founded by the Carolina Power and Light Company and was featured as an "electric" park, having eight thousand electric lights, an electrically powered merry-go-round, a one-third of a mile roller coaster, and a penny arcade with automatic moving pictures and talking machines. In addition, the park held a dancing pavilion, where a band played each summer season. For a nickel, you could take an open air trolley car to the park from Capitol Square.

Bloomsbury Park stayed open for only a few years. At first the park was very popular, but by 1920 it had long passed its peak, and its existence had ended by the early twenties. The merry-go-round was moved to Pullen Park.

Roller Coaster
Bloomsburg Park
Raleigh, N.C.

Courtesy of Duke University Manuscript Department

The trolley car station at Bloomsbury, which was in
what is now the Country Club Hills area.

Courtesy of Duke University Manuscript Department

Land for the first courthouse on Fayetteville Street was donated by James Bloodworth and Theophilus Hunter. Bloodworth's deed stipulated that when the property no longer held a courthouse, it would revert to his heirs. The Wake County Courthouse has been located on this site on Fayetteville Street since 1795.

The first courthouse on Fayetteville Street was a wooden structure which gave way in 1837 to a two-story brick building which was enlarged in the 1880s, and the third courthouse, shown here, was completed in 1915.

Courtesy of Duke University Manuscript Department

In 1966, a 6.6 million dollar bond issue was passed for the construction of the fourth Wake County Courthouse at the Fayetteville Street site. The present structure was designed by Holloway-Reeves and Olsen Associates.

Courtesy of the County Manager's Office

Presented to the state in 1915, this monument, done by Augustus Lukeman, was erected to honor the North Carolina Women of the Confederacy. It was placed upon the southwest corner of Union Square, facing Morgan Street.

Courtesy of the North Carolina Collection

A welcome for the 113th Field Artillery of
the American Expeditionary Forces, on Fayetteville
Street, upon the close of World War I.

Courtesy of North Carolina State Archives

Troops passing through Raleigh receive refreshment from Red Cross volunteers at the railroad station, which stood to the west of Nash Square.

Courtesy of North Carolina State Archives
From the Albert Barden Collection

During the war they were known as Liberty Bonds, but after the war they were called Victory Bonds. The drive was conducted before the Post Office Building.

Courtesy of North Carolina State Archives

An excellent photo taken in 1927 of the old Union
Depot which was located to the west of Nash Square.

Courtesy of North Carolina State Archives

At Pullen Park, about 1920.

Courtesy of North Carolina State Archives

The California Fruit Store was the unlikely name of
Raleigh's favorite ice cream parlor from
about 1910 through to the forties. Here is where you
would go after the movies or after a dance
at the High School. The store also sold fresh
California pineapples, peaches, oranges, and other fruits.

Courtesy of North Carolina State Archives

All of these people were being treated for dog bites
at the State Laboratory of Hygiene. This
1918 photograph was used in the campaign for more
strictly enforced "dog laws."

Courtesy of the North Carolina State University Archives

Members of the 120th Infantry Division march down Fayetteville Street in this photo taken in the early twenties.

Courtesy of Raleigh News and Observer

The photograph has been titled "Hauling Cotton." Heading west on Hillsborough Street, these farmers have been traveling through Raleigh on the way to having their cotton ginned, February 4, 1921.

Courtesy of North Carolina State University Archives

This 1917 photograph shows the Lassiter Mill, and on the right the Lassiter Lumber Mill. In 1936, Cornelius Jesse Lassiter sold the lumber mill to his son Otha N. Lassiter.

Courtesy of Mrs. J. B. Watkins

A display of the Lassiter Mill products, as photographed about 1950.

Courtesy of Mary V. Lassiter and
Durham Herald and Sun

The 1921 class of civil engineering students from State stood for this picture at Lassiter's Mill on Crabtree Creek. Some of the students are wearing campaign hats of the type that was worn by cavalry soldiers. In later years, the State Highway Patrol adopted this kind of hat.

The first mill at this site was built in the 1760s. Through most of the nineteenth century, the mill was owned by Durrel Rogers and his son Isaac H. Rogers, and so the mill was known as Rogers' Mill. Cornelius Jesse Lassiter bought the mill site in 1908, and after that time it was known by his name. Lassiter would tell his children that when he was a boy, he would be allowed only two biscuits on Sundays, and so he determined to someday own a mill.

The Lassiter Mill burned in 1958, though Mary V. Lassiter, daughter of Cornelius Jesse Lassiter, kept the warehouse open until 1975, when it too burned.

Courtesy of North Carolina State Archives

The Confederate Soldiers Home is shown where it stood
off New Bern Avenue in the first decade of
this century.

Courtesy of Raleigh Chamber of Commerce

The old Confederate Soldiers Home used to be on
New Bern Avenue, and this early 1920s photo shows,
from left to right, Wiley T. Johnson, James J. Lewis, and
W. Bert Royster, soldiers of the Confederate Fife
and Drum Corps. Boys of less than fighting age
were used in this corps, and as the war went on, soldiers
in the Fife and Drum Corps became younger
and younger.

Courtesy of North Carolina State Archives

"Wakestone," the Josephus Daniels Home, still stands
at the intersection of Wade Avenue and Glenwood
Avenue. It is now used by the Order of Masons.
     Raleigh, by the way, is the home of the
world's smallest United States Naval Base.
When Josephus Daniels retired from his post as
Secretary of the Navy, he requested that he be given
a naval gun to be mounted before his house. The Navy
was quite willing to comply with his wish, but
discovered that such a gun could only be mounted on an
official United States Navy base. To remedy the
situation, a small plot on Daniels' lawn was designated
as an official Navy base, and the gun was mounted.

Courtesy of North Carolina State Archives

The May Pole Dance at Saint Mary's, on
May Day, 1927.

Courtesy of Saint Mary's College

Football at State in the mid-nineteen-twenties. At
this stage of the game's development, some
players wore helmets, and some did not.

Courtesy of the North Carolina Collection

1922, bayonet training at Riddick Field on the State College campus. The buildings visible in the background, from left to right, are Pullen Hall, Leazar Hall, Holladay Hall, Watauga Hall, the YMCA building, Fourth Dorm, and Syme Hall.

At Peace.

Courtesy of Frank Sherwood

Yates Mill, south of town, was a favorite spot for
an afternoon outing through the twenties and thirties.
Folks would come out and bring their picnic
baskets. Boats could be rented for rowing and fishing.

Courtesy of North Carolina State Archives

The Raleigh High School was built in 1908. Raleigh's
first publicly educated high school students
graduated from this school which stood on Morgan
Street. This photo dates to the late 1920s. The Raleigh
High School burned and was taken down in 1932.

Courtesy of North Carolina State Archives

Needham B. Broughton High School was constructed in
1929 upon twenty-seven acres at a cost of more
than six hundred thousand dollars. The path
that stretches across this photo is said to have been
the forerunner of Peace Street. The school's namesake,
Needham B. Broughton, was a prominent figure in the
Raleigh community; he was a printer, and he was
active as a campaigner for the Democratic party.
Broughton worked zealously to secure the advantages of
public education for the young people in the
community and in the state. He died in 1914.

Courtesy of Needham B. Broughton High School

Raleigh's motorcycle police force of 1929 posed
for this picture before the Davie Street side of the
municipal building. From left are George Peebles, Paul
Cooper, B.M. Spence, and Claude Johnson. In those
times, the police would present an annual show at the
public auditorium in order to raise money for the city.
The policemen would participate in a drill revue,
and then they would take part in more frolicsome events,
such as trying to climb a greased pole.

Courtesy of the Raleigh Police Department

With their hats and overcoats, stand the members of
the Raleigh detective force in 1929. In the front
row, from right, are Captain R. M. Saunders, Lester
Chalmers, Joe Lowe, H. L. Peebles, and L. C. Thompson.
In the second row, from right, are Willie E. Mangum,
Bob Danieley, W. A. Gattis, Will Banks, A. L. Bailey, and
Bud Pearce.

Courtesy of the Raleigh Police Department

Fayetteville Street, in the aftermath of the snow.
Courtesy of the North Carolina Collection

New Bern Avenue after the Snow of '27.
Courtesy of the North Carolina Collection

March of 1927 produced one of the worst snowstorms in the history of the state. When the storm was over, Raleigh was covered by snow. Most everyone stayed inside; most every business stayed closed. But as you can see, Governor McLean had his lunch packed, put on his boots, and came in to work. You can also see that someone else did a little shoveling.

Courtesy of the North Carolina Collection

The fire which destroyed the Yarborough House in 1928. Hudson-Belk now stands on the former site of this hotel. In its day, the Yarborough House provided accommodations for President Theodore Roosevelt, Howard Taft, and Woodrow Wilson. Once, at the Yarborough House, an attractive woman with an engaging manner was arrested and charged with being a German spy, and she was taken away to Washington.

Courtesy of the North Carolina Collection

The Wake County Courthouse is visible behind the ruins of the Yarborough House in this photo taken after the fire.

Courtesy of North Carolina State Archives

Raleigh's Josephus Daniels is often remembered today as the founder of the *News and Observer*, though in fact he bought the already existing newspaper. In the 1920s, editor Daniels was able to crusade rather successfully against corruption in the state government.

Daniels served as Secretary of the Navy under Woodrow Wilson. He was the first to admit women into the armed forces in positions and ranks equal to those held by men. He also forbade the use of liquor in Navy officers' clubs, causing a furor among some of the staff, but he made this ruling stick.

Courtesy of North Carolina State Archives

A look at North Blount Street, just beyond Peace
Street, shortly before the time of World War I.

Courtesy of North Carolina State Archives

A closer look at the Raney House which stood near
the corner of Hillsborough and Salisbury Streets, and
which was taken down in recent years.

Courtesy of North Carolina State Archives

illsboro Street, Raleigh N. C.

RALEIGH
AUG 24
5-30P

Gracious Hillsborough Street as photographed from
the Capitol grounds about the time of World War I.
The Raney House is the first on the right side of the
street, and next to it is the Johnson House. The spire
of the Edenton Street Methodist Church can be seen
behind the Johnson House, and the Catholic Church
is in view farther down Hillsborough Street.

Courtesy of North Carolina State Archives

From the 1920s to the 1940s, the Parker House was especially noted as a fine place for out-of-towners to come for lodgings and a Southern dinner. Uncle Charles, who was well thought of in town, would wear a white coat and give a dignified greeting.

Courtesy of North Carolina State Archives

The Parker House, an interior view.

Courtesy of North Carolina State Archives

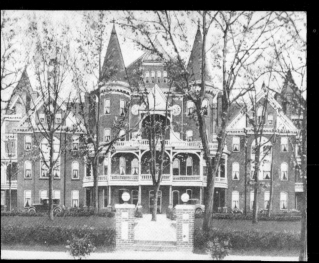

After the burning of the Yarborough House, the Sir Walter Hotel began to receive that hotel's political clientele. The Sir Walter has accommodated presidents and foreign dignitaries. Connie Mack and his Philadelphia Athletics would stay at the Sir Walter, and at least one hotel employee who was there in those days attests to playing late night games of dice with the ballplayers. Tom Mix came to Raleigh and stayed at the Sir Walter. He did bring his horse to town, but "Tony" stayed elsewhere.

Courtesy of North Carolina State Archives

The now-demolished Meredith College main building, serving, by the time of this 1929 photograph, as the Mansion Park Hotel.

Courtesy of North Carolina State Archives

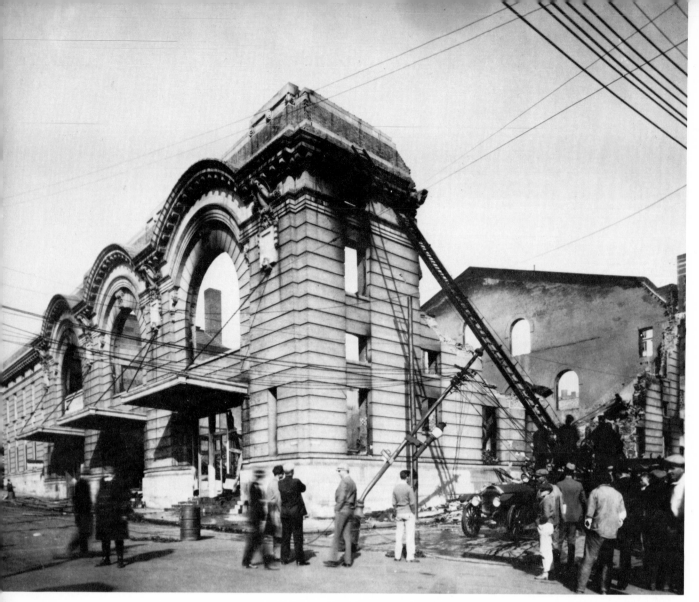

A fire started shortly before midnight on October 24, 1930, brought down the city auditorium. Believed to have been started from careless smoking in the men's locker room, the flames were fanned by a brisk northwest wind, and the building was quickly destroyed. The Wilmington Street side of the building collapsed, bringing down power lines, but without damaging other nearby property. Damage to the city hall annex of the building was limited, caused by water and falling bricks and not by the fire itself.

Courtesy of North Carolina State Archives

Raleigh's Memorial Auditorium was built in 1932. It was renovated in 1963, and can now seat over four thousand. For many years, the Governor's Inauguration was traditionally held at Memorial Auditorium. It is now the home of the North Carolina Symphony.

Courtesy of the North Carolina Collection

On stage at the 1934 Chevrolet Show are Jimmy Poyner and his Collegians. At one time, Les Brown played with this band. The singers from right to left are Jimmy Poyner, George Poyner, and Key Scales. Kenlon Brockwell is on bass, Furman Betts at the piano, Carroll Oldham has the guitar, and Johnny Feather is on drums. The winds, from right to left, are Ray White, Johnny McLain, Shimmy Harris, and Teem Palms, with Lewis Curry in back. Another member of the band, not in the photo, was Jimmy Gerow.

Courtesy of Kenlon H. Brockwell

The crowd has turned out for the dedication
ceremonies of the Raleigh Municipal Airport in 1929.
The "City of Raleigh," an Armed Forces plane,
was later christened after having flown in from
New York.

Courtesy of North Carolina State Archives

This 1938 photograph shows the Manhattan Lunch, which was favored by students at State, and which was also frequented by Raleigh's best known tramp, Pud Lucas, who, in turn, favored the State students with his shuffling and singing. Lucas lived on tips from his clog-dancing. He wore brogans, and sometimes, several overcoats. In 1932 he devised one of his best-known shuffles: shuffling up and then back, he would sing, "Roosevelt coming in, Hoover coming out."

Courtesy of North Carolina State Archives

The Palace Theater on Martin Street. Vitaphone was the forerunner of the talkies. At this time, the movies were among the most popular and talked about forms of entertainment for the people of Raleigh, as they were for the people of the entire country. The comedy serials were great favorites, especially in the early twenties, and one such serial, pleasantly recalled, was *Neil of the Navy*. Neil's adventures and misadventures could be followed at the Alamo Theater with a weekly expenditure of five cents.

Many, many Raleigh homes of this time had pianos, and an evening would often be spent in the parlor, while some might engage themselves in a game of set-back if they didn't wish to go to the pictures.

Courtesy of Raleigh News and Observer

Improvements upon the Capitol grounds, 1934. Benches no longer line the west side of the grounds.

Courtesy of North Carolina State Archives

Visitors
As the Capital of North Carolina, Raleigh has received many, many famous visitors. Here are but a few of them.

Teddy Roosevelt spoke at the State Fair in 1905, and the people of Raleigh responded warmly to his presence. "Delighted," he would say on making an acquaintance.

Courtesy of Raleigh News and Observer

In 1907 Carrie Nation came and spoke against the evil of drink. She is shown with S. J. Betts.

Courtesy of North Carolina State Archives

Presidential Candidate Al Smith was here in September of 1928.

Courtesy of North Carolina State Archives
From the Albert Barden Collection

Will Rogers arrives, on October 28, 1932. America's most loved humorist is shown with Mrs. Josephus Daniels at the airport.

Courtesy of North Carolina State Archives
From the Albert Barden Collection

The Democratic Candidate of 1928, Al Smith, was defeated by the Republican Herbert Hoover. But with the onset of economic depression, the nation was eager for a change in government. Franklin Delano Roosevelt came to Raleigh in the course of his successful Presidential Campaign in 1932, and spoke, as was his habit, from the back of a railroad car.

Courtesy of North Carolina State Archives

In 1947, General Eisenhower met with North Carolina State University Chancellor Harrelson and Governor Cherry in the Governor's Office.

Courtesy of North Carolina State University Archives

Harry S. Truman came to town in 1948 and made a stop at the State Fair. From left are Governor J. Melville Broughton, Fair Manager Dr. J. S. Dorton, President Truman, Senator Willis Smith, Commissioner of Agriculture David S. Coltraine, and the last member of the group was not identified.

Courtesy of North Carolina State Archives

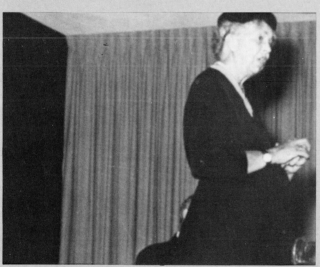

Eleanor Roosevelt spoke to a group at State.

Courtesy of North Carolina State University Archives

Lyndon Johnson met the people at Reynolds Coliseum in 1964.

Courtesy of North Carolina State Archives

"The old mud hole" was transformed into a Drama Center through the combined efforts of the Raleigh Little Theatre, the city, and the WPA. Construction of the center was approved as a Labor Project by the federal government in 1938. The Raleigh Little Theatre is now in its fortieth year. This year a new stage has been added at the center for the "Theatre Downstairs," which is used for off-Broadway and small-cast productions.

Courtesy of Ron Campbell

Hmmh...

Plead as he may, it seems to be too late for the fellow in the white hat, Fitzhugh Dade. Adamant in their decision are Mary Alice Spivey, Ainslie Prior, and James Thiem, in *Dream Girl,* presented at the Raleigh Little Theatre in October, 1947.

The photograph shows Tatton Hall, built during the
thirties in impressive Georgian fashion on Oberlin Road.

Courtesy of North Carolina State Archives

Fayetteville Street, 1938.

Courtesy of North Carolina State Archives

Pullen Park, 1938.

Courtesy of North Carolina State Archives

Master William P. Beaty buys a Defense Bond with his own savings, on December 8, 1941, the day following the "day of infamy." He is shown with Mr. Haynes of the Raleigh Industrial Bank.

Courtesy of North Carolina State Archives

A truckload of food, donated by State students, was gathered by the members of the Monogram Club and the Golden Chain, December 3, 1941. William Friday, wearing the hat, became President of the Consolidated University of North Carolina in 1956. Rimless glasses, like those worn by two students in this photo, have recently become popular again.

Courtesy of North Carolina State University Archives

ROTC students at State take target practice on
Wednesday, December 3, 1941.

Courtesy of North Carolina State University Archives

These two photographs from the North Carolina State
University Archives provide glimpses of the effects of
World War II within Raleigh. In the first photograph,
Professor George Bauerlein, Jr. is registering freshman
Frank Craven for the selective service.

The second photograph was taken on October 7,
1942, and on that day the college organized a scrap metal
round-up. Enough scrap metal was gathered in two hours
and forty-five minutes to fill three railroad freight cars.

Courtesy of North Carolina State University Archives

Races were held between Fire Stations Five and One on August 3, 1943. Station Five prevailed. In the photo are firemen Oscar Green, Jack Biggs, Bryan Davis, C. G. Mumford, Walton Dennis, Sam Ruauk, S. T. Ballenger, C. L. Greaves, F. H. Jeter, Rupert Atkins, J. P. Lowery, Stan Hassinger, Bob Warren, Leroy Jay, and Gene Knight.

Courtesy of Walton S. Dennis

Until recent years the High School and minor league baseball games had been held at the Devereaux Meadow Park, located off Peace Street. This nighttime photo probably dates to the early forties.

Courtesy of North Carolina State Archives

It has been said that before Everett Case came to Raleigh to coach the North Carolina State University basketball team, a field goal was thought to be worth three points. In his first ten years at State, his teams would win two hundred and sixty-seven games while losing only sixty. These teams would win six straight Southern Conference tournaments and three consecutive Atlantic Coast Conference tournaments. In the photograph, Case is shown standing before the framework of Reynolds Coliseum. Construction of the coliseum was halted during World War II, when steel was no longer available. Since its completion in 1949, more fans have come to Reynolds to watch college basketball than have come to any other campus arena.

Courtesy of the North Carolina State University Athletic Department

An aerial view of downtown Raleigh
taken from behind Memorial Auditorium
in 1946. It is hard to believe that the
heart of the city's downtown section was
heavily residential such a short time ago.

Courtesy of North Carolina State Archives

The Raleigh Country Club was opened in 1948, and
this photograph was taken shortly after that time. The
club, right, was located just beyond the eastern city
limits, though over the years Raleigh has grown to
extend beyond the club.

Courtesy of the North Carolina Collection

This photograph, taken on December 11, 1949, shows
the St. Mary's Christmas pageant which was
traditionally held in the chapel.

Courtesy of North Carolina State Archives

The Raleigh High School Band, October 14, 1949.

Courtesy of North Carolina State Archives

The birthday celebration of City Manager Roy Braden was photographed on April 2, 1949. Among those in the photo are Annabelle Weeks, Tom Willis, Tom Hobbs, J. B. Lambeth, Fire Chief Lloyd, Robert Goodwin, W. C. Gatling, J. D. Duncan, Herbert Hayes, and W. R. Price.

Courtesy of Ethel Young

Bishop Edwin A. Penick spoke at the dedication of
Penick Hall on the Saint Augustine's College campus
in 1950. Penick was Bishop of the Diocese of North
Carolina and was Chairman of the Board of Trustees
of Saint Augustine's. College President Harold Trigg is
shown wearing the formal robe.

Courtesy of North Carolina State Archives

The Chapel of Saint Augustine's College, as
photographed in 1949.

Courtesy of North Carolina State Archives

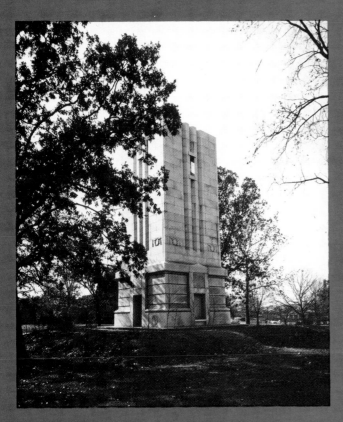

State's Memorial Tower grew in several stages. It is shown as it appeared in 1927, and then as it appeared about 1950. A plaque inside the Tower's Shrine Room, which commemorates the school's World War I dead, originally bore the name George L. Jeffers. Jeffers, an alumnus of the school, was wounded during the war, but he did recover from his injuries. It was first thought that he had died and so his name was inscribed on the plaque. When the mistake was discovered, the name George E. Jeffers was changed to the fictitious name George E. Jefferson.

Courtesy of the North Carolina Collection

Fayetteville Street in the early fifties.
Courtesy of North Carolina State Archives

In the window at the Ivey-Taylor Store in 1952 was a collection of hats that were in vogue between 1910 and 1918.

Courtesy of North Carolina State Archives

On this desk, Charles W. Dabney wrote the proposal for the Agriculture and Mechanic College.
Legislation calling for the establishment of the school was passed in 1887, and the school was opened in the fall of 1889. In this 1952 photograph, Agricultural Commissioner L. Y. Ballentine gives the desk key to North Carolina State University's Chancellor J. W. Harrelson. Dean Emeritus I. O. Schaub attends the presentation.

Courtesy of North Carolina State University Archives

Mr. W. H. Kelly, eighty-eight years of age, settles with a book brought to him by the Olivia Raney Library's Bookmobile.

Courtesy of the Olivia Raney Library

"Sir William Pepperelle and his Family" can be seen in the Art Gallery Lobby. It was done in 1778 by John Singleton Copley, who is often described today as the best of the early American portrait painters. Both Copley and his subject, Pepperelle, were Bostonians who moved to London.

Courtesy of North Carolina Museum of Art

In 1947, the North Carolina legislature authorized the appropriation of one million dollars for the "purchase of an art collection for the state," and this marked the first time a state government in this country had ever made such an appropriation. It was stipulated that the amount be matched by an outside donation, and the Samuel H. Kress Foundation more than fulfilled this requirement with a gift of early Italian Renaissance paintings and other European art works. Originally an office building of the Highway Department, the museum was opened in 1956.

Courtesy of North Carolina Museum of Art

Coleman Jenkins, Queen of the May Day celebration, is shown, with her court, on the Saint Mary's campus in 1957. Court members include Dickie Robinson, Octavia Phillips, and Marjorie Coddington.

Courtesy of Saint Mary's College

The Research Triangle Park grew from three universities, the University of North Carolina, Duke University, and North Carolina State University. This joining of resources and effort marks a coming trend in research and enterprise. Since its inception in 1957, the Triangle has become world-renowned as a center of scientific advancement. In recent years it has provided more stimulus to the growth of Chapel Hill, Durham, and Raleigh than has any other institution or factor.

Courtesy of the Research Triangle Institute

The J. S. Dorton arena was a pioneer effort in the field of architectural design; the structure was one of the first to be built using the combined forces of compression and tension. Matthew Nowicki, head of the Department of Architecture at North Carolina State University, planned the three hundred feet in diameter elliptical arena. In 1950, before the building was constructed, Nowicki was killed in an airplane crash, and his friend, the architect William Henly Deitrick of Raleigh, was named to the project.

Courtesy of J. S. Dorton Arena

Twenty-eight feet in diameter is the terrazzo mosaic of the Great Seal of the State of North Carolina which adorns the podium before the State Legislative Building. The state motto, *Esse Quam Videri,* means "To Be Rather than to Seem."

Courtesy of the North Carolina Collection

North Carolina's State Legislative Building, facing
onto Jones Street, holds both the Senate and the
House, committee rooms, and offices. Upon its
completion in 1963, it became the first building in this
country specifically constructed to serve a state
legislature. The entire structure rests upon a broad
podium of North Carolina granite that measures 340
feet in width. Of modern styling, the structure designed
by Edward Durrel Stone maintains a classic sense
of unity.

Courtesy of the Division of Travel and Promotion
Photo by Clay Nolen

The Senate and the House.

Courtesy of the Division of Travel and Promotion
Photos by Clay Nolen

This photograph taken from the Seaboard Building shows the State Administration Building which faces onto Jones Street. It houses the Offices of the Governor and the offices of the Secretary of State, the Department of the State Auditor, and the Department of Administration and other state agencies.

Courtesy of the Division of Travel and Promotion
Photo by Clay Nolen

Part of this building on Caswell Square served to hold the old State School for the Blind. It is now used as the Office of Water and Air Resources of the Department of Natural and Economic Resources, and it stands in distinct contrast with the other modern government buildings on Jones Street.

This classroom building on the State campus has been
named for John Harrelson, Dean of Administration
from 1934 to 1945, and Chancellor from 1945 until
1953. Its circular design is unusual for an academic
structure, and was chosen to make maximum use of the
limited space available. In essence, the building is
composed of concentric circles about a core, outer
circles of offices, the circular corridors, and the inner
circles of classrooms. On each floor the outer circle of
offices is higher than the inner circle of classrooms, so
that all the floors of the Harrelson Building, one
above the other, may be thought of as a "stack of
soup plates."

Photo by Todd Huvard

Colonel Polk built his home just beyond the north
boundary of the city. The Marquis de Lafayette
breakfasted there on a visit to Raleigh, and Henry
Clay once stopped at the Polk House. In 1872, the
house was moved because it blocked the northward
extension of Blount Street, and it was moved to its
last location in 1903. The Colonel Polk home at 1100
Harp Street was brought down by fire in February,
1975.

Courtesy of Raleigh News and Observer

The Colonel William Polk house is shown as it appeared in the fall of 1967. When no longer used as a residence, the house intermittently held a civic center and several small shops.

Courtesy of North Carolina State Archives

Having served as a colonel in the American Revolution, the patriot William Polk was a popular figure in Raleigh's early days. Polk was a founder of the Society of Cincinnati, the first President of the State Bank, and a trustee of the University of North Carolina. A staunch Federalist, Polk's popularity waned within the young city when he opposed the nationalists who sought the war of 1812.

Courtesy of North Carolina State Archives

Raleigh's new Civic Center will be located at the foot
of the Downtown Mall, and at the projected time of
its completion, in 1978, it will be ready to house a
wide variety of activities, from dances and banquets to
conventions and trade shows to sporting events. The
Center's arena will seat over four thousand, and an
adjacent assembly area will be designed to hold three
thousand. The Center's outdoor plaza will lend itself to
the presentation of open-air concerts. Architects for
the project are Odell Associates Inc., of Charlotte, and
Haskins and Rice of Raleigh.

*Courtesy of Odell Associates Incorporated
and Haskins and Rice*

The Blount Street Historic District includes the Andrews-Duncan House at the northwest corner of Blount and North Streets.

Courtesy of North Carolina State Archives

The Vass House was built at the corner of Edenton and Halifax Streets in the 1880s by a former President of the Raleigh-Gaston Railroad, William Vass. It was a fine example of the extravagant and complex Victorian architectural era, and the house had survived until the very last few years.

Courtesy of North Carolina State Archives

Upon defeating UCLA in the championship game, State's team members and coaches line up with their trophy. With State's fine basketball program honed by competition in the Atlantic Coast Conference, hopes for another national crown will rise with every coming year. In the first row from right are Head Coach Norm Sloan, Monte Towe, Moe Rivers, Bruce Dayhuff, and Assistant Coach Art Musselman. In the second row are Assistant Coach Eddie Biedenbach, David Thompson, Greg Hawkins, Dwight Johnson, Craig Kuszman, and Assistant Coach Sam Esposito, and in the back row are Steve Nuce, Tom Burleson, Tim Stoddard, Mike Buurma, Mark Moeller, Phil Spence, Bill Lake, and managers Biff Nichols and Mike Sloan (hidden).

Courtersy of the North Carolina State
University Athletic Department
Photo by Ed Caram

State's 1973-74 basketball season was crowned by the winning of the National College Athletic Association championship. Seven foot, four inch Tommy Burleson and David Thompson were the leaders of State's championship team. Burleson is standing while the six foot, four inch Thompson is shown leaping high in the air to block a shot by University of California at Los Angeles six foot, eleven inch center, Bill Walton. Superlative after superlative was used by sportswriters to describe Thompson's astounding jumping ability. Notice the players on the UCLA bench.

Courtesy of the North Carolina State
University Athletic Department
Photo by Ed Caram

Fayetteville Street as it appeared in 1972.

Courtesy of North Carolina State Archives

The "Downtown Mall" is now in the making and is expected to be completed by the spring of 1977. It will include lawns, trees, pools and fountains, courtyards, sculpture, and a clock and bell tower. The project of designing the mall has been undertaken by the Raleigh firm of Dodge and Beckwith Architects.

Drawing by William W. Dodge, III

Fayetteville Street, 1976. Raleigh's most busily
trafficked byway over the years is open only to
pedestrians; an era has ended. Has an era ended or
does time wind back upon itself? In about 1885, before
Fayetteville Street was paved, the General Assembly,
descrying the muddy condition of the city's main artery,
jokingly passed a bill to charter a ferry to travel up

The State Laboratory of Hygiene was established in 1905 to examine the public drinking water supply and to diagnose communicable diseases. The lab was first located above a store on Fayetteville Street.

Nowadays, the Bath Building, pictured here, houses the Laboratory of Hygiene as well as other concerns of the State Health Service.

Courtesy of the Division of Travel and Development
Photo by Clay Nolen

Named for one of the original North Carolina Counties, which no longer exists, the Archdale Building will house the Department of Natural and Economic Resources. Presently under construction and expected to be completed by 1977, the Archdale Building was designed by the architectural firm Odell Associates, Inc., of Charlotte.

Courtesy of Odell Associates, Incorporated

The Hollywood Cafe' on Martin Street facing Nash Square still features a marble counter-top, something now not often seen. When the Cafe' was opened forty-five years ago, a steak cost fifty cents.

Photo by Jackson Hill

Peace College at night.

Photo by Todd Huvard

Briggs Hardware, as it is known to Raleigh today and as it has been known for more than a century, was started from the partnership of T. H. Briggs and James Dodd in 1865. They began in a small shop and built this store building which was still used in 1874. In this time, Dodd quit the partnership, and the business became T. H. Briggs and Sons. The Briggs building itself is nearly symbolic of the city's history; its exterior remains as it was when built.

Photo by Jackson Hill

Crabtree Valley Shopping Center is the fourth largest of such retail centers in the southeast.

Photo by Todd Huvard

Todd Huvard photographed the Raleigh skyline at dusk from Dix Hill.

A section of the Blount Street sidewalk was
photographed in front of the Heck-Andrews House.
Attention to such details is often neglected in the
present day.

The Holiday Inn looms above the Dodd-Hinsdale
House, showing a clear contrast in the architectural
fashions of two different centuries. The two buildings
stand side by side in downtown Raleigh, and their
nearness demonstrates that the present city exists as a
combination of the old and the new.

Crabtree Creek.

Photo by Todd Huvard

At Moore Square.

Photo by Terry Cantrell

At Capitol Square.

Photo by Terry Cantrell

The Boylan Street Bridge, constructed 1913.
What is what is passed?
It would have no bearing, no mooring, no rudder,
If it did not pertain to what is.

> William Henry Wordsworth,
> "Lines composed a Few Miles
> above Tintern Abbey"

While with an eye made quick by the power of
harmony, and the deep power of joy,
We see into the life of things.

Photo by Jackson Hill